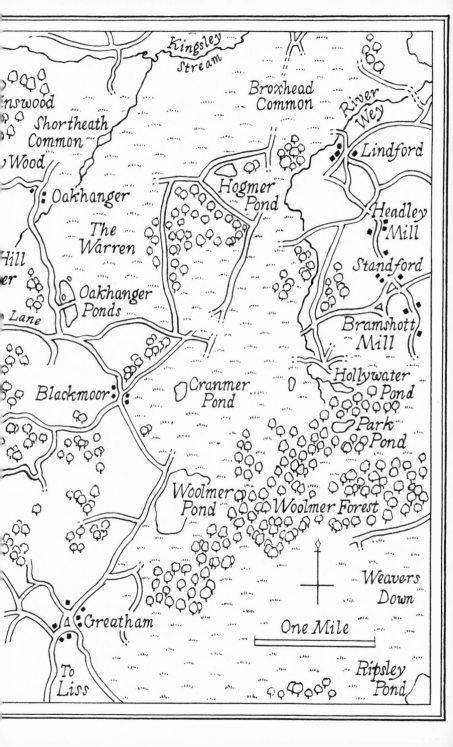

GILBERT WHITE

Passages from
*THE NATURAL HISTORY
OF SELBORNE,
NATURALIST'S JOURNAL*
and other writings

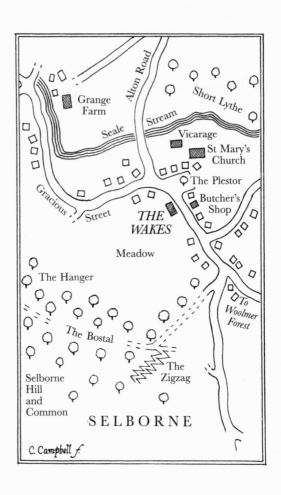

GILBERT WHITE

Passages from
*THE NATURAL HISTORY
OF SELBORNE,
NATURALIST'S JOURNAL*
and other writings

Wood engravings by
THOMAS BEWICK

Selected and introduced by
COLIN CAMPBELL

SILENT BOOKS · *CAMBRIDGE*

First published in Great Britain 1993
by Silent Books, Swavesey, Cambridge CB4 5RA

Introduction and this selection © Colin Campbell 1993

ISBN 1 85183 051 0

British Library Cataloguing-in-Publication Data.
A catalogue record for this book is available from the
British Library.

Typeset by Textype Typesetters, Cambridge
Printed in Great Britain at The Alden Press, Oxford

GILBERT WHITE, who published only one book in his lifetime, would not have regarded his work as writing in any literary sense. Yet his *Natural History and Antiquities of Selborne* (1789), known all over the world in more than two hundred editions and translations, is the only publication of its kind to be acclaimed as a classic. What is the secret of this naturalist's enduring popularity? White's posthumous fame is guaranteed by the qualities that enabled him to communicate with readers who are not themselves naturalists: modesty, humour, vividness of imagery, unaffected simplicity of style, and an affection for nature in its 'minute particulars'. Today, when the language of science has become cold and technical, these qualities have more appeal than ever.

Born in 1720, White was educated at a school in Basingstoke and at Oxford University. After ordination in 1749 he held a succession of minor posts before becoming curate in his native Selborne, a beautiful village within earshot of the 'sweet peal of bells at Farnham' which is situated in the folds of the chalk hills where Hampshire adjoins Surrey and Sussex. A gentle, kindly man, he took a genuine interest in the welfare of his parishioners, many of whom were employed on local farms and hop-gardens. But his parochial duties were far from arduous, leaving him plenty of time to study, improve his house and grounds, and enjoy the company of the friends and relations whose visits cheered his bachelor existence.

It was rare for events in the outside world to impinge upon the lives of the inhabitants of secluded Selborne. Jean

Blanchard caused a stir when he sailed over the village in a balloon in October 1784; but the moment he was gone Selborne returned to its own affairs. On occasion, these could be out of the ordinary: a mad dog once went berserk in the main street, and seventeen people, fearing rabies, were taken in a waggon to be dipped in the sea. But life was generally uneventful, the shape and character of each day governed by humdrum, predictable routines. A wet day at 'The Wakes', White's home, might find the curate making mushroom ketchup, supervising the redecoration of his parlour, helping a nephew with a translation of Horace, or sending to London for green tea and sealing-wax. If the weather was fine, White would be in the garden, marking his annuals for seed or testing the temperature of his melon-beds.

White's passion for gardening is documented by his *Garden Kalendar*, a daily record of horticultural activities begun in 1751 and continued until the end of the following decade. The *Kalendar* reveals the practical importance of a regular supply of fruit and vegetables to a clergyman of limited means, but White's methods were also experimental. Gardening led to botany, and White's researches in this area can be found in the meticulous *Flora Selborniensis* compiled during the twelve months of 1766. Botanizing was accompanied by the study of natural history, and in 1768 White began making notes in a *Naturalist's Journal* on the flora and fauna that the diverse topography of Selborne and its environs supported. In this journal, which White kept until a few days of his death in 1793, data on barometric pressure and weather are combined with field observations on subjects ranging from the diet of hedgehogs to the migration of birds. Its pages contain remarks on horticultural activities (the *Garden Kalendar* having been discontinued), and it also refers to domestic circumstances, the farming year, and goings-on in the village. But it is essentially a naturalist's notebook, and as such it formed an important source for the letters to Daines Barrington and the zoologist Thomas Pennant that were ultimately published in the *Natural History of Selborne*.

The examples of observation, analysis and reflection in this anthology have been extracted from all White's writings: the journals, the *Natural History of Selborne*, and private correspondence. Although they touch on a wide range of subjects, topics such as the swallow and the harvest-mouse in which White made notable contributions to natural science have received due emphasis. The passages have been arranged under the days of the year on which they (or the passages to which they are thematically linked) were written, or else under the days of the year to which they refer. The system follows both that of the composite journal White devised for his projected *Annus historico-naturalis* and the selection of entries from White's journals which Dr John Aikin published in 1795 as *A Naturalist's Calendar*. Besides being a logical arrangement for dated texts that deal with topics of seasonal significance, the system allows the quotation of many memorable passages that would normally be excluded from an anthology on grounds of brevity. It also provides a means of bringing together comments on any given subject which, to the frustration of the modern reader, are scattered in White's writings. If the result reads like a conventional journal, this is mainly because the pattern of the seasons and White's related activities changed little from one year to the next.

The Tyneside artist Thomas Bewick (1753–1828), who had developed engraving on boxwood into a medium capable of naturalistic representation by the late 1780s, would have been a far more suitable choice of illustrator for the first edition of the *Natural History of Selborne* than the copper-plate engraver Peter Mazell. A naturalist in his own right, Bewick's work is informed by White's wit, sympathy and eye for the unexpected. Some amends for the missed opportunity are made here. White's writing (which Bewick read) does not of course *need* illustration, and this is why Bewick's tailpieces have been chosen in preference to his portrait-like headpieces. The intention is to *complement* rather than illustrate the text. These tiny engravings (all reproduced actual size) are the perfect accompaniment to White, echoing as they do the latter's most original achievement. As in the vignettes that White created with words, Bewick's vignettes depict animals and birds as part of the totality of a living, vital nature to which we ourselves also belong.

JANUARY

January 1

Snow in the night.

January 2

Fierce frost, sun, deep snow.

Grey and white wagtails appear every day: they never leave us.

All the species of wagtails in severe weather haunt shallow streams near their spring-heads, where they never freeze; and, by wading, pick out the aurelias [pupae] of the genus of *phryganae*, etc.

January 3

Rime hangs on the trees all day.

At eight o'clock in the evening Captain Lindsey's hands were frozen, as he and Mr. Powlett were returning from Captain Dumery to Rotherfield. The gentleman suffered pain all night, and found his nails turned black in the morning. When he got to Rotherfield he bathed his hands in cold water.

January 4

Meat freezes so hard it can't be spitted.

We were much obliged to the thermometers for the early

information they gave us: and hurried our apples, pears, onions, potatoes, etc. into the cellar and warm closets; while those who had not, or neglected such warnings, lost all their stores of roots and fruits, and had their very bread and cheese frozen.

January 5

The fierce drifting of Wednesday proved very injurious to houses, forcing the snow into the roofs, and flooding the ceilings. The roads also are so blocked up with drifted snow that the coaches cannot pass. The Winton coach was overturned yesterday near Alresford.

January 6

The snow on Wednesday proved fatal to two or three people, who were frozen to death on the open downs about Salisbury. Much damage happened at sea about that time. In particular, the Halsewell outerbound Indiaman was wrecked, and lost on the shore of Purbeck.

January 7

Robert Berriman has lost by his illness two horses very lately; and now his cow, which by some strange neglect got into the barn's floor in the night, and gorged herself so at an heap of threshed wheat, that she died what they call *sprung*, being blown up to a vast size. These accumulated losses amount, it is supposed, to full £27!

January 8

Received five gallons and seven pints of French brandy from Mr. Comd. Woods.

January 9

Titmice pull straws from the eaves.

Every species of titmouse winters with us . . . The great titmouse, driven by stress of weather, much frequents houses, and, in deep snows, I have seen this bird, while it hung with its back downwards (to my no small delight and admiration), draw straw lengthwise from out the eaves of thatched houses, in order to pull out the flies that were concealed between them, and that in such numbers that they quite deface the thatch, and gave it a ragged appearance. The blue titmouse, or nun, is a great frequenter of houses, and a general devourer. Beside insects, it is very fond of flesh; for it frequently picks bones on dunghills: it is a vast admirer of suet, and haunts butchers' shops. When a boy, I have known 20 in a morning caught with snap mouse-traps, baited with tallow or suet. It will also pick holes in apples left on the ground, and be well entertained with the seeds on the head of a sunflower. The blue, marsh, and great titmice will, in very severe weather, carry away barley and oat straw from the sides of ricks.

January 10

T[imothy] Turner has sunk his well nine feet without coming

to water. He now desists on account of the expense. My well, I now find, has more than three feet of water; but the rope is too short to reach it.

January 11

Hares frequent the garden and nibble the pinks.

The sun has scarce appeared for many days . . . The Thames, it seems, is so frozen, that fairs have been kept on it; and the ice has done great damage to the ships below bridge.

January 12

A cock pheasant appears at the dunghill at the end of my stable; tamed by hunger.

January 13

Vast frost-work on the windows.

Poultry do not stir out of the hen-houses: they are amazed, and confounded in snow, and would soon perish. Hares lie by at first, till compelled to beat out by hunger.

January 14

Rugged, Siberian weather.

January 15

The frost, where a grave was dug, appeared to have entered the ground about 12 inches.

January 16

Hedge-sparrows frequent sinks and gutters in hard weather, where they pick up crumbs and other sweepings . . . Redbreasts and wrens in the winter haunt outhouses, stables and barns, where they find spiders and flies that have laid themselves up during the cold season. But the grand support of the soft-billed birds in winter is that infinite profusion of aurelias of the *lepidoptera ordo*, which is fastened to the twigs of trees and their trunks; to the pales and walls of gardens and buildings; and is found in every cranny and cleft of rock or rubbish, and even in the ground itself.

January 17

Hens chatter for laying.

Of all the occurrences of their life, that of laying seems to be the most important; for no sooner has a hen disburdened herself than she rushes forth with a clamorous kind of joy, which the cock and the rest of his mistresses immediately adopt. The tumult is not confined to the family concerned, but catches from yard to yard, and spreads from every homestead within hearing, till at last the whole village is in an uproar.

January 18

From the 14th the snow continued to increase, and began to stop the road waggons and coaches, which could no longer keep on their regular stages; and especially on the western roads, where the fall appears to have been deeper than in the south. The company at Bath, that wanted to attend the Queen's birthday, were strangely incommoded: many carriages of persons who got, in their way to town from Bath, as far as Marlborough, after strange embarrassments, here met with a *ne plus ultra.* The ladies fretted, and offered large rewards to labourers if they would shovel them a track to London; but the relentless heaps of snow were too bulky to be removed, and so the 18th passed over, leaving the company in very uncomfortable circumstances at the Castle and other inns.

January 19

Received from London a quarter of an hundred [weight] of salt-fish.

January 20

Lambs fall, and are frozen to the ground.

Mr. Hool's man says that he caught this day, in a lane near Hackwood Park, many rooks which, attempting to fly, fell from the trees with their wings frozen together by the sleet, that froze as it fell.

January 21

Flocks of wild geese pass over.

January 22

The snowdrops are in bloom, and the crocus swelling.

We have had all this winter 26 highlanders of the 77th Regiment quartered in this village, and at Oakhanger: where, though they had nothing in the world to do, they have behaved in a very quiet and inoffensive manner; and were never known to steal even a turnip, or a cabbage, though they lived much on vegetables, and were astonished at the dearness of southern provisions. Late last night came an express ordering these poor fellows down to Portsmouth, where they are to embark for India.

January 23

Sun, spring-like, bright. Boys play on the Plestor [village green] at marbles and peg-top. Thrushes sing in the coppices. Thrushes and blackbirds are much reduced.

Made an hotbed on the dunghill in the yard, with Mr. Johnson's frame, for white mustard and cress.

January 24

Long the mason finished the dry wall of the ha-ha in the new garden, which is built of blue ragstone, so massy that it is supposed to contain double the quantity of stone usual in such walls. Several stones reach into the bank 20 inches . . . . An excellent fence against the mead, and so well fastened into the clay bank that it looks likely to stand a long while. The workmanship, exclusive of carting the stones, cost £1 8s 10d.

January 25

Larks rise and essay to sing.

January 26

Rooks resort to their nest-trees.

There is a large rookery round this house, the inhabitants of which seem to get their livelihood very easily; for they spend the greatest part of the day on their nest-trees when the weather is mild. These rooks retire every evening all the winter from this rookery, where they only call by the way, as they are going to roost in deep woods. At the dawn of day they always revisit their nest-trees, and are preceded a few minutes by a flight of [jack]daws that act, as it were, as their harbingers.

January 27

The earth is now full of water, which runs from the fields into the hollow lanes.

Among the singularities of this place [are] the two rocky hollow lanes, the one to Alton, the other to the forest . . . These roads, running through the malm lands, are, by the traffic of ages and the fretting of water, worn down through the first stratum of our freestone, and partly through the second; so that they look more like water-courses than roads; and are bedded with naked rag for furlongs together. In many places they are reduced 16 or 18 feet beneath the level of the fields; and after floods, and in frosts, exhibit very grotesque and wild appearances, from the tangled roots that are twisted among the strata, and from the torrents rushing down their broken sides; and especially when those cascades are frozen into icicles, hanging in all the fanciful shapes of frost-work. These rugged gloomy scenes affright the ladies when they peep down into them from the paths above, and make timid horsemen shudder while they ride along them; but delight the naturalist with their various botany, and particularly with their curious *filices* [ferns] with which they abound.

January 28

Several slow-worms found under the bottom of an old hayrick in a torpid state, but not without some motion.

January 29

The dung and litter freezes under the horses in the stable. The hares nibble off the buds on the espalier pear-trees.

January 30

Sent for 42 bushels of peat-ashes from the forest side . . . . Brought at the same time an old sandstone roller from Mr. Bridger's at Oakhanger. It was, it seems, formerly the property of Mr. Xmass of Oakhanger, father to Sarah Xmass; and may probably have been made these 60 or 70 years, and yet is very little damaged by age or weather.

January 31

Vast halo round the moon.

FEBRUARY

February 1

On this cold day about noon a bat was flying round Gracious Street pond, and dipping down and sipping the water like swallows as it flew: all the while the wind was very sharp, and the boys were standing on the ice!

February 2

Brown wood-owls [tawny owls] come down from the Hanger in the dusk of the evening and sit hooting all night on my walnut-trees.

February 3

In the evening of February 3rd the sheep were ravenous after their hay, and before bedtime came a great flight of snow with wind. Sheep are desirous of filling their bellies against bad weather, and are by their voraciousness prognostic of that bad weather.

February 4

The imbecility [physical weakness] of birds seems not to be the only reason why they shun the rigour of our winters; for the robust wryneck (so much resembling the hardy race of woodpeckers) migrates, while the feeble little golden-crowned wren [goldcrest], that shadow of a bird, braves our severest frosts without availing himself of houses or villages, to which most of our winter birds crowd in distressful seasons, while this keeps aloof in the fields and woods; but perhaps this may be the reason why they may often perish, and why they are almost as rare as any bird we know.

As to the matter of long-billed birds growing fatter in moderate frosts, I have no doubt within myself what should be the reason. The thriving at those times appears to me to arise altogether from the gentle check which the cold throws upon insensible perspiration. The case is just the same with blackbirds, etc.; the farmers and warreners observe, the first, that their hogs fat more kindly at such times, and the latter that the rabbits are never in such good case as in a gentle frost. But when frosts are severe, and of long continuance, the case is soon altered, for then a want of food soon overbalances the repletion occasioned by checked perspiration. I have observed, moreover, that some human constitutions are more inclined to plumpness in winter than in summer.

February 5

The missel-thrush, or storm-cock, sings on the great oak in the meadow.

February 6

Grey, sun, spring-like. Bees gather on the snowdrops. Flies come out in the windows.

February 7

Brewed 45 gallons of strong beer with eight bushels of malt dried with Welsh coal; and three pounds and three-quarters of good hops. The strong beer was closely covered down with sacks, while infusing in the mash vat: and the yeast was beat into the beer several times, till it was put into the barrel. Made with the same malt half an hogshead of ale, and an hogshead of small [beer]. The strong beer was made entirely with rain water. Tunned the strong beer the third day.

February 8

Venus shadows very strongly, showing the bars of the windows on the floors and walls.

February 9

Vast rain in the night, with some thunder and hail. Peter Wells's well runs over.

Tubbed and pickled a fat porker: weight nine scores and 11 pounds: price eight shillings and four pence from Farmer Hoar.

February 10

Sheep rot very much. Ewes and lambs are much distressed by the continual wet.

Turkey-cock struts and gobbles.

February 11

Eruptive fevers and sore throats lurk about the parish: some die of this disorder.

February 12

My musical friend, at whose house I am now visiting, has tried all the owls that are his near neighbours with a pitchpipe, set at concert pitch, and finds that they all hoot in B flat. He will examine the nightingales next spring.

February 13

Foxes begin now to be very rank, and to smell so high that as one rides along of a morning it is easy to distinguish where they have been the night before. At this season the intercourse between the sexes commences, and the females intimate their wants to the males by three or four little sharp yelpings or barkings frequently repeated.

February 14

Showers, showers with hail, showers. A perfect and lovely rainbow.

February 15

Made half an hogshead of raisin-wine with one hundred of Malagas, and half an hundred of Smyrnas. One basket of the Smyrnas were pretty much candied, the rest were pretty good. Put to the raisins 12 buckets of water, each bucket containing three gallons.

February 16

House-sparrows get in clusters, and chirp and fight.

Sent some winter-aconites in bloom to Dr. Chandler, and received back some roots of *arum dracunculus* [dragon plant].

February 17

Bees rob each other and fight.

February 18

Men plough and sow.

February 19

Insects come forth.

February 20

We have had a strange wedding lately. A young mad-headed farmer out of Berks came to marry Farmer Bridger's daughter, and brought with him four drunken companions. He gave two guineas and a crown to the ringers; and came and drank with them, and set all the village for two days in an uproar . . . These heroes, after they had drank all the second day in the Compasses, while a dinner dressing at the great farm at Newton was spoiled, went up at last, and ranted and raved so, that they drove the two Mrs. Hammonds (one of whom is the bride's eldest sister) up into their chambers through fear. At six in the evening they took the bride (who wept a good deal) and conveyed her away to Berks.

February 21

Yesterday I fixed some nuts in the chinks of some gate-posts in a part of my outlet where nuthatches used to haunt, and today I found that several of them were drilled, and the kernels gone.

There are three creatures, the squirrel, the field-mouse and the bird called the nuthatch (*sitta Europaea*), which live much on hazel nuts; and yet they open them each in a different way. The first, after rasping off the small end, splits the shell in two with his long foreteeth, as a man does with his knife; the second nibbles a hole with his teeth, so regular as if drilled with a wimble, and yet so small that one would wonder how the kernel can be extracted through it; while the last picks an irregular ragged hole with its bill: but as this artist has no paws to hold the nut firm while he pierces it, like an adroit workman, he fixes it, as it were in a vice, in some cleft of a tree, or in some crevice; when, standing over it, he perforates the stubborn shell.

February 22

The hazel, *corylus sylvestris*, blowing [blooming], with vast numbers of their male catkins opening which give the hedges a yellow tinge.

February 23

Mr. White of Newton sprung a pheasant in a wheat-stubble and shot at it; when, notwithstanding the report of the gun, it was immediately pursued by the blue hawk, known by the name of hen harrier, but escaped into some covert. He then sprung a second and a third in the same field, that got away in the same manner: the hawk hovering round him all the while that he was beating the field, conscious no doubt of the game that lurked in the stubble. Hence we may conclude that this bird of prey was rendered very daring and bold by hunger and that hawks cannot always seize their game when they please. We may further observe that they cannot pounce their quarry on the ground, where it might be able to make a stout resistance; since so large a fowl as a pheasant could not but be visible to the piercing eye of an hawk, when hovering over a field. Hence that propensity of cowering and squatting till they are

almost trod on, which no doubt was intended as a mode of security, though long rendered destructive to the whole race of *gallinae* by the invention of nets and guns.

February 24

Made a cucumber-bed full 14 feet long, and almost four feet deep at the back for my two two-light frames with 10 dung-carts of dung . . . Covered the dung the space of one of the frames about five inches thick with tan, and filled a deep hole in the centre of each light with the same. Laid a leaden pipe into the frame that has got a tin chimney . . . in order to convey in a succession of fresh air a-nights.

February 25

A pair of house-pigeons, which were hatched at Michaelmas last, now have eggs and sit. An instance of early fecundity!

What pigeons in a state of nature may do I cannot pretend to say; but this I know, that tame pigeons, which are pampered by high feeding and lie perhaps under more frequent temptations from living together in crowds, are apt to forget the rules of strict chastity, and follow too often the example of people in high life.

February 26

Our butcher began to kill grass-lamb.

February 27

Vast storm. Had the duration of this storm been equal to its strength, nothing could have withstood its fury. As it was, it did prodigious damage. The tiles were blown from the roof of Newton Church with such violence that shivers from them broke the windows of the great farmhouse at near 30 yards distance.

February 28

Dew, sun, sweet day. Bumble-bees, and many *muscae* [flies] appear. Spiders shoot their webs from clod to clod.

Frogs swarm in the ditches. Spawn.

February 29

Remarkable vivid *aurora borealis.*

MARCH

March 1

Sent a large flitch of bacon to be dried in Mr. Etty's chimney [smoke-loft]. It lay seven weeks and three days in salt on account of the frost, during which it did not seem to take salt.

March 2

Farmer Parsons sows wheat in his fallow behind Beacher's shop, which was drowned in the winter. Mem.: to observe what crop he gets from this spring sowing.

March 3

Helleborus foetidus, stinking hellebore . . . all over the High Wood and Coneycroft Hanger. This continues a great branching plant the winter through, blossoming about January, and is very ornamental in shady walks and shrubberies. The good women give the leaves powdered to children troubled with worms; but it is a violent remedy and ought to be administered with caution.

March 4

Great distress among the flocks: the turnips are all rotten, the ewes have little milk, and the lambs die.

March 5

Boys play at hop-scotch and cricket.

Tunned the raisin-wine, which held out exactly, leaving about a gallon for filling up. Coloured it with twelve bottles of elder syrup and put to it one quart of brandy.

March 6

Rooks build.

Rooks, in the breeding season, attempt sometimes in the gaiety of their hearts to sing, but with no great success.

March 7

Glazier's bill . . . £2 5s 10d for garden-lights and hand-glasses.

March 8

In the night between the 8th and 9th . . . a considerable part of the great woody hanger at Hawkley was torn from its place, and fell down, leaving a high freestone cliff naked and bare, and resembling the steep side of a chalk-pit. It appears that this huge fragment, being perhaps sapped and undermined by waters, foundered, and was engulfed, going down in a perpendicular direction; for a gate which stood in the field, on the top of the hill, after sinking with its posts for thirty or forty feet, remained in so true and upright a position as to open and shut with great exactness, just as in its first situation. Several oaks also are still standing, and in a state of vegetation, after taking the same desperate leap . . . About an hundred yards from the foot of this hanging coppice stood a cottage by the side of the lane; and two hundred yards lower, on the other side of the lane, was a farmhouse in which lived a labourer and his family; and, just by, a stout new barn. The cottage was inhabited by an old woman and her son and his wife. These people in the evening, which was very dark and tempestuous, observed that the brick floors of their kitchens began to heave and part; and that the walls seemed to open, and the roofs to crack . . . The miserable inhabitants, not daring to go to bed, remained in the utmost solicitude and confusion, expecting every moment to be buried under the ruins of their shattered edifices. When daylight came, they were at leisure to contemplate the devastations of the night: they then found that a deep rift, or chasm, had opened under their houses, and torn them, as it were, in two; and that one end of the barn had suffered in a similar manner; that a pond near the cottage had undergone a strange reverse, becoming deep at the shallow end, and so *vice versa*; [and] that many large oaks were removed out of their perpendicular.

March 9

Mr. Mill, the clergyman at Farringdon, appeared against the smuggler that robbed him on the Farnham road, and has got him condemned: he is a most daring fellow, and has twice broken out of gaol, once at Dorchester, and once at Winton.

Cock turkey struts, and makes love.

March 10

Vast tempest all night and this morning; which at noon blew down the weathercock on the [church] tower.

Plashed, and banked up the quickset hedge between Turner's and the orchard. Planted hollyhocks in the new garden. Sowed poppy-seed and larkspur seed in the borders of the new garden. Dressed asparagus-beds; earthed up the late row of celery in the field-garden.

March 11

Cellars flooded.

March 12

Rooks are continually fighting and pulling each other's nests to pieces: these proceedings are inconsistent with living in such close community. And yet if a pair offers to build on a single tree the nest is plundered and demolished at once.

Some unhappy pairs are not permitted to finish any nest till the rest have completed their building. As soon as they get a few sticks together, a party comes and demolishes the whole.

March 13

Made a very deep and large hot bed for my melon seeds; etc: with seven cart-loads of dung. Thatched the edges of the bed without the frame.

March 14

Bat appears.

I was much entertained last summer with a tame bat, which would take flies out a person's hand. If you gave it anything to eat, it brought its wings round before the mouth, hovering and hiding its head in the manner of birds of prey when they feed. The adroitness it showed in shearing off the wings of flies, which were always rejected, was worthy of observation, and pleased me much. Insects seem to be most acceptable, though it did not refuse raw flesh when offered: so that the notion that bats go down chimneys and gnaw men's bacon seems no improbable story. While I amused myself with this wonderful quadruped, I saw it several times confute the vulgar opinion that bats when down on a flat surface cannot get on the wing

again, by rising with great ease from the floor. It ran, I observed, with more dispatch than I was aware of; but in a most ridiculous and grotesque manner.

March 15

Sowed two pots of Mr. Garnier's cantaloup melons . . . Carried Mr. Garnier's cantaloup seed (being but two years old) in my breeches pocket six or eight weeks.

March 16

Primroses blow.

March 17

The stone-curlew is returned again; and was heard this evening passing over the village from the uplands down to the meadows and banks.

Birds that fly by night are obliged to be noisy: their notes are signals, or watch-words to keep them together, that they may not stray, and lose each other in the dark.

March 18

The twigs which the rooks drop in building supply the poor with brushwood to light their fires.

March 19

The hunters killed a female hare which gave suck: so there are young leverets already.

March 20

Wonderful is the regularity observed by nature! I have often remarked that the smallest willow wren . . . called here the chiff-chaff from its two loud sharp notes, is always the first spring bird of passage, and that it is heard usually on March 20: when behold, as I was writing this very page, my servant looked in at the parlour door, and said that a neighbour had heard the chiff-chaff this morning!! These are incidents that must make the most indifferent look on the works of Creation with wonder!

March 21

Goose sits, while the gander with vast assiduity keeps guard, and takes the fiercest sow by the ear and leads her away crying.

March 22

Planted in the basons [beds] in the field, a moss-provence, and some damask, Monday, and red roses; *spiraea frutex*; blue and white lilacs; syringa; early golden-rod; sumach; *althaea frutex*; guelder rose; *coccigrya*; female dogwood; double-flowering thorn; and Persian jasmine. In the new garden forward honeysuckle; lavender cotton; golden sage; double and single lychnis; blue and white campanulas; catchflies; blue and peach-bloom Michaelmas daisies; striped bulbous iris; ribbon-grass; double and variegated periwinkle: and fruit-bearing passion-flower near the brew-house door.

March 23

Earth-worms travel about in rainy nights, as appears from their sinuous tracks on the soft muddy soil, perhaps in search of food.

Earth-worms, though in appearance a small and despicable link in the chain of nature, yet, if lost, would make a lamentable chasm. For, to say nothing of half the birds, and some quadrupeds, which are almost entirely supported by them, worms seem to be the great promoters of vegetation, which would proceed but lamely without them, by boring, perforating, and loosening the soil, and rendering it pervious to rains and the fibres of plants, by drawing straws and stalks of leaves and twigs into it; and, most of all, by throwing up such infinite numbers of lumps of earth called worm-casts, which, being their excrement, is a fine manure for grain and grass.

March 24

My nephew John White of Salisbury sent me a fine pike, or jack; it was in high season, full of soft roe, and weighed five pounds and six ounces. The length from eye to fork two feet. It was baked, and much admired when it came on the table.

March 25

John Carpenter has opened a shop with a great bow-window on the Plestor, in which he sells ironmongery, hardware, cheese and breeches.

Tried an experiment late in the evening with a candle on the two cucumber-frames after they had been close covered up some hours. On putting the candle down a few inches into that frame that has leaded lights and no chimney, the flame was extinguished at once three several times by the foul vapour: while the frame with the tiled lights and chimney was so free from vapour that it had no sensible effect on the flame. I then applied the candle to the top of the chimney, from whence issued so much steam as to affect the flame, though not put it out. Hence it is apparent that this invention must be a benefit to plants in hotbeds by preventing them from being stewed in the night-time in the exhalations that arise from the dung and their own leaves.

March 26

Hedge-sparrow has eggs.

March 27

Blackbirds and thrushes lay.

March 28

Soft air. Toads crawl forth.

March 29

The moorhen, or waterhen, *gallinula chloropus major*, chatters and sports in the water.

I planted five fanned elms to screen Will. Carpenter's necessary house [privy], and five large laurels in a curve to screen my own, which I propose to move to the corner next Parson's yard to conceal my own from the street.

March 30

Violets and coltsfoot blow.

Papilio rhamni [brimstone butterfly] sucks the bloom of the primrose.

March 31

Planted four limes in the butcher's yard to hide the sight of blood and filth from the window.

Cellars almost dry by pumping.

APRIL

April 1

Woodlarks hang suspended in the air and sing all night.

April 2

Bees resort to the hotbeds tempted by some honey spread on the leaves and blossoms of the cucumbers. When bees do not frequent the frames the early fruit never sets well.

April 3

Cowslips blow under hedges.

April 4

Though . . . 'to burn on any waste, between Candlemas and Midsummer, any grig, ling, heath and furze, gorse or fern, is punishable with whipping and confinement in the house of correction'; yet, in this forest, about March or April, according to the dryness of the season, such vast heath fires are lighted

39

up that they often get to a masterless head, and, catching the hedges, have sometimes been communicated to the underwoods, woods and coppices, where great damage has ensued. The plea for these burnings is that when the old coat of heath, etc., is consumed, young will sprout up and afford much tender browse for cattle; but, where there is large old furze, the fire, following the roots, consumes the very ground; so that for hundreds of acres nothing is to be seen but smother and desolation, the whole circuit round looking like the cinders of a volcano; and the soil being quite exhausted, no traces of vegetation are to be found for years. These conflagrations, as they take place usually with a north-east or east wind, much annoy this village with their smoke, and often alarm the country.

April 5

The air smells very sweet and salubrious.

A very large fall of timber of about 1,000 trees has been cut this spring in the Holt Forest; one fifth of which belongs to the grantee, Lord Stawell. He lays claim also to the lop and top: but the poor of the parishes of Binstead and Frensham say it belongs to them and have actually in a riotous manner taken it away. One man that keeps a team has carried home near 40 stacks of wood. 49 of these people his Lordship has served with actions; and provided they do not make restitution, proposes to sue them.

April 6

Many flies are out basking in the sun.
  Young goslings on [the] commons.

April 7

Dark sun, harsh wind. The blackthorn begins to blow. This tree usually blossoms while cold north-east winds blow, so that the harsh, rugged weather obtaining at this season is called by the country people blackthorn winter.

April 8

Lapwings haunt the down.

April 9

Planted five rows of large fine potatoes, with a layer of peat-dust in every trench. Sowed a crop of carrots, parsnips, cos lettuce and onions; a plot of leeks; double-stocks, dwarf sunflowers and savoys.

April 10

It appears from good information that sometimes the osprey, *falco haliaetus* Linnaeus, is known to haunt the great pond at Frensham. It darts down with great violence on a fish, so as to plunge itself quite under water. The man at the ale-house adjoining shot one as it was devouring its prey on the handle of a plough.

April 11

Soft rains . . . Shell-snails come out in troupes.
  Ivy-berries are ripe. The birds eat them and stain the walks with their dung.

April 12

In the night between the 11th and 12th of this month [John] Burbey's shop was attempted. The assailants wrenched off the hinges at the bottom of the shutters, and so crept up between the shutters and the sash, and broke the glass; and with a knife began to cut and hack, in a very bungling way, the bars of the sash. It is imagined that they were disturbed in their business by some means, for they never got in, nor could reach to the *till*, which is near the window, and was, it is supposed, the object they had in view. Burbey heard the glass jingle; but being half awake, did not know what was the matter.

April 13

I went to the sheep-down, where the ring-ouzels have been observed to make their appearance at spring and fall, in their way perhaps to the north or south; and was much pleased to see three birds about the usual spot. We shot a cock and a hen; they were plump and in high condition. The hen had but very small rudiments of eggs within her, which proves they are late breeders; whereas those species of the thrush kind that remain with us the whole year have fledged young before that time . . . I dressed one of these birds and found it juicy and well-flavoured.

April 14

Swallow, *hirundo domestica*, returns.

Mr. Ventris observed at Farringdon a little whirlwind which

originated in the road before his house, taking up the dust and straws that came in its way. After mounting up through one of the elms before the yard and carrying away two of the rooks' nests in which were young squabs; it then went off, leaving the courtyard strewed with dust and straws, and scraps of twigs, and the little naked rooks sprawling on the ground. A pair of rooks belonging to one of these nests built again, and had a late brood.

April 15

Hot sun, muddy sky . . . . Timothy the tortoise roused himself from his winter slumbers and came forth. He was hidden in the laurel hedge under the walnut-tree, among the dead leaves.

April 16

Green woodpecker laughs at all the world.

April 17

Hay is become very scarce and dear indeed! My rick is now almost as slender as the waist of a virgin; and it would have been much for the reputation of the two last brides that I have married, had their waists been as slender.

April 18

This morning I saw the gold-crowned wren, whose crown glitters like burnished gold.

April 19

Bright, sun and gale, flisky clouds.
Pulled down the old martins' nests against the brew-house and stable: they get foul and full of vermin. These abounded

with fleas . . . Besides, while these birds are *building* they are much more in sight, and are very amusing.

April 20

Several swallows, house-martins and bank-martins play over Oakhanger ponds. The horses wade belly deep over those ponds to crop the grass floating on the surface of the water.

Set the old Bantam speckled hen with eleven eggs. My cookmaid desired there might be an odd egg for good luck . . . *numero Deus impare gaudet* [odd numbers please God].

April 21

Timothy begins to eat: he crops the daisies, and walks down to the fruit-wall to browse on the lettuces.

No part of [this tortoise's] behaviour ever struck me more than the extreme timidity it always expresses with regard to rain; for though it has a shell that would secure it against the wheel of a loaded cart, yet does it discover as much solicitude about rain as a lady dressed in all her best attire, shuffling away on the first sprinklings, and running its head up in a corner. If attended to, it becomes an excellent weather-glass; for as sure as it walks elate, and as it were on tiptoe, feeding with great earnestness in a morning, so sure will it rain before night.

April 22

In a church-yard of this village is a yew-tree, whose aspect bespeaks it to be of a great age: it seems to have seen several centuries, and is probably coeval with the church, and therefore may be deemed an antiquity: the body is squat, short, and thick, and measures 23 feet in the girth, supporting a head of suitable extent to its bulk. This is a male tree, which in spring sheds clouds of dust, and fills the atmosphere around with its farina . . . . In a yard, in the midst of the street, till very lately, grew a middle-sized female tree of the same species,

which commonly bore great crops of berries. By the high winds usually prevailing about the autumnal equinox, these berries, then ripe, were blown down into the road, where the hogs ate them. And it was very remarkable, that, though barrow-hogs and young sows found no inconvenience from this food, yet milch-cows often died after such a repast: a circumstance that can be accounted for only by supposing that the latter, being much exhausted and hungry, devoured a larger quantity. While mention is making of the bad effects of yew-berries, it may be proper to remind the unwary, that the twigs and leaves of yew, though eaten in a very small quantity, are certain death to horses and cows, and that in a few minutes.

April 23

Cuckoo sings on the hill.

A boy has taken three little young squirrels in their nest, or drey as it is called in these parts. These small creatures he put under the care of a cat who had lately lost her kittens, and finds that she nurses and suckles them with the same assiduity and affection as if they were her own offspring .... Thus hens, when they have hatched ducklings, are equally attached to them as if they were their own chickens.

April 24

The fruit-wall and espalier trees are all alive, and begin to shoot.

April 25

Distant thunder, and fine showers.

The lightning on Friday morning shivered the masts of the *Terrible* man-of-war on Portsmouth Harbour.

April 26

A pair of nightingales haunt my fields: the cock sings nightly in the Portugal laurel, and Balm of Gilead fir.

April 27

Oaks are felled: the bark runs freely.

April 28

Put sticks to the peas. Weeded and thinned the lettuce.

The uplands glow with pile-worts and dandelions; the wet meadows with marsh-marigolds.

April 29

Hanger almost in full leaf.

A sprig of *antirrhinum cymbalaria*, the ivy-leaved toadflax, which was planted last year on a shady water-table of the wall of my house, grew at a vast rate and extended itself to full *nine* feet; and was in perpetual bloom till the hard frost came. In the severity of the winter it seemed to die; but it now revives again with vigour and shows the rudiments of flowers. When in perfection it is a lovely plant.

April 30

Cucumbers now come by heaps.

Tied those hyacinths that are white with pink eye with a piece of scarlet worsted as a mark to save offsets from. Marked the blue hyacinths with a blue piece of worsted tied to the sticks that stand before them.

MAY

May 1

A pair of [tree-]creepers (*certhia*) built at one end of the parsonage house at Greatham behind some loose plaster. It is very amusing to see them run creeping up the walls with the agility of a mouse. They take great delight in climbing up steep surfaces; and support themselves in their progress with their tails, which are long, and stiff and inclined downwards.

May 2

Disbudded some of the vines.

My left hand is full of gout: all my fingers look red, and shoot and burn. If I have gout about me it is best to come out.

May 3

A pair of missel-thrushes have made a nest in the apple-tree near the fruit-wall. One young half-fledged was found in the garden.

May 4

The King and Queen are this day at Portsmouth to see the fleet at Spithead. There were five general running firings, which shook my house and made the windows jar.

Hay is now risen to four pounds per ton. No grass in the fields, and great distress among the cattle.

Goody Hampton came to work in the garden for the summer.

May 5

Fine growing weather.

May 6

Cut the stalks of garden-rhubarb to make tarts.

May 7

The orchard is mown for the horses.

May 8

Made an annual bed with grass-mowings and sowed it with African and French marigolds, pendulous amaranthus and China asters. Sowed some snapdragon seeds and some dwarf sunflowers. Planted five short rows of globe artichokes, sent me by Mr. Fort of Salisbury.

49

May 9

Master Trimming is taken with the smallpox.

The magpies, which probably have young, are now very ravenous and destroy the broods of missel-thrushes, though the dams are fierce birds and fight boldly in defence of their nests. It is probably to avoid such insults that this species of thrush, though wild at other times, delights to build near houses, and in frequented walks and gardens.

May 10

The Bantam hen hatches seven chickens.

May 11

The down of willows floats in the air, conveying, and spreading about their seeds, and affording some birds a soft lining for their nests.

Added a pint more of brandy, in all five pints, to the last raisin-wine, which still hisses pretty much.

May 12

The sycamore or great maple is in bloom, and at this season makes a beautiful appearance, and affords much *pabulum* for bees, smelling strongly like honey.

May 13

The rain last night broke the stems of several of the tulips, which are in full bloom.

When the rain is considerable, swifts skim with their wings inclining, to shoot off the wet.

May 14

Swallows build. They take up straws in their bills, and with them a mouthful of dirt.

The swallow, though called the chimney-swallow, by no means builds altogether in chimneys, but often within barns and outhouses against the rafters . . . Here and there a bird may affect some odd, peculiar place; as we have known a swallow build down the shaft of an old well . . . but in general with us this *hirundo* breeds in chimneys; and loves to haunt those stacks where there is a constant fire, no doubt for the sake of warmth. Not that it can subsist in the immediate shaft where there is a fire; but prefers one adjoining to that of the kitchen, and disregards the perpetual smoke of that funnel, as I have often observed with some degree of wonder. Five or six or more feet down the chimney does this little bird begin to form her nest about the middle of May, which consists, like that of the house-martin, of a crust or shell composed of dirt or mud, mixed with short pieces of straw to render it tough and permanent; with this difference, that whereas the shell of the martin is nearly hemispheric, that of the swallow is open at the top, and like a deep dish. This nest is lined with fine grasses, and feathers which are often collected as they float in the air. Wonderful is the address which this adroit bird shows all day long in ascending and descending with security through so narrow a pass. When hovering over the mouth of the funnel, the vibrations of her wings acting on the confined air occasion a rumbling like thunder. It is not improbable that the dam submits to this inconvenient situation so low in the shaft in order to secure her broods from rapacious birds, and particularly from owls, which frequently fall down chimneys, perhaps in attempting to get at these nestlings.

May 15

Caught a mouse in the hotbed.

Sheared my dog, Rover, and made use of his white hair in plaster for ceilings. His coat weighed four ounces. The north-east wind makes Rover shrink.

May 16

A pair of house-martins began building their nest against my brew-house.

About the middle of May, if the weather be fine, the martin begins to think in earnest of providing a mansion for its family. The crust or shell of this nest seems to be formed of such dirt or loam as comes most readily to hand, and is tempered and wrought together with little bits of broken straws to render it tough and tenacious. As this bird often builds against a perpendicular wall without any projecting ledge under, it requires its utmost efforts to get the first foundation firmly fixed, so that it may safely carry the superstructure. On this occasion the bird not only clings with its claws, but partly supports itself by strongly inclining its tail against the wall, making that a fulcrum; and thus steadied it works and plasters the materials into the face of the brick or stone. But then, that this work may not, while it is soft and green, pull itself down by its own weight, the provident architect has prudence and forbearance enough not to advance her work too fast; but by building only in the morning, and by dedicating the rest of the day to food and amusement, gives it sufficient time to dry and harden. About half an inch seems to be a sufficient layer for a day. Thus careful workmen when they build mud walls (informed perhaps by this little bird) raise but a moderate layer at a time, and then desist; lest the work should become top-heavy, and so be ruined by its own weight. By this method in about 10 or 12 days is formed an hemispheric nest with a small aperture towards the top – strong, compact and warm.

May 17

Timothy Turner's Bantam sow brings 20 pigs, some of which she trod on and overlaid, so that they were soon reduced to 13. She has but 12 teats. Before she farrowed, her belly swept the ground.

May 18

Dandelions are going out of bloom; and now the pastures look yellow with the *ranunculus bulbosus*, buttercups.

May 19

Many pairs of daws build in the church: but they have placed their nests so high up between the shingles and the ceiling that the boys cannot come at them.

[An] unlikely spot is made use of by daws as a place to breed in, and that is Stonehenge. These birds deposit their nests in the interstices between the upright and the impost stones of that amazing work of antiquity: which circumstance alone speaks the prodigious height of the upright stones, that they

should be tall enough to secure those nests from the annoyance of shepherd-boys, who are always idling round that place.

May 20

The thunder of this evening burnt the barns and outhouses of a farm between Gosport and Tichfield, and destroyed eight fine horses.

May 21

Laurel and lilac blossom. *Apis longicornis* [wild-bee] appears over the grass-walks, in which they bore holes.

May 22

Lily of the valley blows.

We have lost poor Timothy, who, being always in a great bustle in such hot weather, got out, we suppose, at the wicket, last Thursday, and is wandered we know not whither!

May 23

[Spotted] flycatcher builds in the vine.

The flycatcher . . . builds every year in the vines that grow on the walls of my house. A pair of these little birds had one year inadvertently placed their nest on a naked bough, perhaps in a shady time, not being aware of the inconvenience that followed. But an hot sunny season coming on before the brood was half-fledged, the reflection of the wall became insupportable and must inevitably have destroyed the tender young had not affection suggested an expedient and prompted the parent birds to hover over the nest all the hotter hours, while with wings expanded and mouths gaping for breath, they screened off the heat from their suffering offspring.

May 24

The turtle-dove, *turtur*, cooes.

May 25

An old hunting-mare, which ran on the common, being taken very ill came down into the village as it were to implore the help of men, and died the night following in the street.

May 26

The grasshopper-lark [grasshopper-warbler] whispers all night.

Nothing can be more amusing than the whisper of this little bird, which seems to be close by though at an hundred yards distance; and, when close at your ear, is scarce any louder than when a great way off . . . The country people laugh when you tell them that it is the note of a bird. It is the most artful creature, skulking in the thickest part of a bush; and will sing at a yard distance, provided it be concealed. I was obliged to get a person to go on the other side of the hedge where it haunted; and then it would run, creeping like a mouse, before us for a hundred yards together, through the bottom of the thorns; yet it would not come into fair sight: but in a morning early, and when undisturbed, it sings on the top of a twig, gaping and shivering with its wings.

May 27

Discovered the rudiments of a wasp's nest: it had 10 cells complete, three of which were each furnished with a single egg. Killed the breeding-wasp that belonged to it, which was very large.

Wasps make their nests with the raspings of sound timber; hornets with what they gnaw from decayed. These particles of wood are kneaded up with a mixture of saliva from their own bodies, and moulded into combs.

May 28

Timothy found in the little bean-field short of the pound-field.

He had conceived a notion of much satisfaction to be found in the range of the meadow and Baker's Hill; and that beautiful females might inhabit those vast spaces, which appeared boundless in his eye. But having wandered till he was tired, and having met with nothing but weeds and coarse grass and solitude, he was glad to return to the poppies and lettuces and other luxuries of the garden.

May 29

My weeding-woman swept up on the grass-plot a bushel basket of blossoms from the white apple-tree, and yet that tree seems still covered with bloom.

May 30

Barn-owls are out in the day, taking their prey in the sunshine about noon.

The young of the barn-owl are not easily raised, as they want a constant supply of fresh mice: whereas the young of the brown owl will eat indiscriminately all that is brought; snails, rats, kittens, puppies, magpies, and any kind of carrion or offal.

May 31

My whitethorn, which hangs over the earth-house, is now one sheet of bloom, and has pendulous boughs down to the ground.

JUNE

June 1

Men wash their fatting sheep, and bay the stream to catch trouts.

John Carpenter brings home from the Plasket at Rotherfield some old chestnut-trees which are very long. In several places the woodpeckers had begun to bore them. The timber and bark of these trees are so very like oak as might easily deceive an indifferent observer; but the wood is very shakey, and towards the heart cup-shakey, that is to say, apt to separate in serried pieces like cups, so that the inward parts are of no use. They were bought for the purpose of cooperage, but must make but ordinary barrels, buckets, etc. Chestnut sells for half the price of oak; but has sometimes been sent into the King's docks and passed off instead of oak.

June 2

Many sorts of dragonflies appear for the first time. Swifts devour the small dragonflies as they take their flight from out their aurelias, which are lodged on the weeds of ponds.

Flag-iris and orange-lily begin to blow. The forward wheat undulates before the wind.

June 3

Honeysuckles are beautiful and fragrant.

Myriads of tadpoles traverse Combe Wood Pond in shoals.

June 4

Bees swarm.

We had in this village more than 20 years ago an idiot boy, whom I well remember, who, from a child, showed a strong propensity to bees; they were his food, his amusement, his sole object. And as people of this cast have seldom more than one point of view, so this lad exerted all his few faculties on this one pursuit. In the winter he dozed away his time, within his father's house, by the fireside, in a kind of torpid state, seldom departing from the chimney corner; but in the summer he was all alert, and in quest of his game in the fields, and on sunny banks. Honey-bees, humble-bees and wasps were his prey wherever he found them: he had no apprehensions from their stings, but would seize them *nudis manibus*, and at once disarm them of their weapons, and suck their bodies for the sake of their honey-bags. Sometimes he would fill his bosom between his shirt and his skin with a number of these captives; and sometimes would confine them in bottles. He was a very *merops apiaster*, or bee-bird; and very injurious to men that kept bees; for he would slide into their bee-gardens and, sitting down before the stools, would rap with his finger on the hives, and so take the bees as they came out. He has been known to overturn hives for the sake of honey, of which he was passionately fond . . . . As he ran about he used to make a humming noise with his lips, resembling the buzzing of bees.

This lad was lean and sallow, and of a cadaverous complexion; and, except in his favourite pursuit, in which he was wonderfully adroit, discovered no manner of understanding.

June 5

The caterpillars of some *phalaenae* [moths] abound on the foliage of the apricots, which they tie together with their webs, and gnaw and deface in a bad manner. We wash the trees with the garden-engine.

June 6

Swifts abound; near 15 pairs.

In the longest days [they do] not withdraw to rest till a quarter before nine in the evening, being the latest of all day birds. Just before they retire whole groups of them assemble high in the air, and squeak, and shoot about with wonderful rapidity.

The redstart sits singing on the vane of the maypole, and on the weathercock of the tower.

June 7

Field-cricket makes its shrilling noise.

There is a steep abrupt pasture field interspersed with furze close to the back of this village, well known by the name of the Short Lythe, consisting of a rocky dry soil, and inclining to the afternoon sun. This spot abounds with the *gryllus campestris* or field-cricket . . . Sitting in the entrance of their caverns they chirp all night as well as day from the middle of the month of May to the middle of July; and in hot weather, when they are most vigorous, they make the hills echo; and, in the stiller hours of darkness, may be heard to a considerable distance. In the beginning of their season, their notes are more faint and inward; but become louder as the summer advances, and so die away again by degrees. Sounds do not always give us pleasure according to their sweetness or melody; nor do harsh sounds always displease. We are more apt to be captivated or disgusted with the associations which they promote, than with the notes themselves. Thus the shrilling of the field-cricket, though sharp and stridulous, yet marvellously delights some hearers, filling their minds with a train of summer ideas of everything that is rural, verdurous, and joyous.

June 8

Sun, perfect summer's day.

Sowed a pint more of dwarf kidney-beans in the room of those that were devoured by snails.

June 9

Horse-chestnut begins to bloom.

Thrushes do great service in hunting out the shell-snails in the hedges and destroying them. The walks are covered with their shells.

June 10

The laburnums are in bloom, and high beauty.

Myriads of mayflies appear for the first time on the Alresford stream. The air was crowded with them, and the surface of the water covered. Large trouts sucked them in as they lay struggling on the surface of the stream, unable to rise till their wings were dried.

June 11

Elder begins to blow. When the elder blows out the summer is at its height.

My niece Hannah's squirrel is much delighted with the fruit of the coniferous trees, such as the pine, the fir, the larch, and

the birch; and, had it an opportunity, would probably be pleased with the cones of alders. As to Scotch firs [Scotch pines], squirrels not only devour the cones, but they also bark large boughs and gnaw off the tops of the leading shoots; so that the pine groves belonging to Mr. Beckford at Basing Park are much injured and defaced by those mischievous quadrupeds, which are too subtle and too nimble to be easily taken or destroyed.

June 12

Sheep are shorn.

June 13

The bloom of the vines fills the chambers with an agreeable scent somewhat like that of mignonette.

June 14

White butterflies innumerable: woe to the cabbages!

June 15

A pair of partridges haunt Baker's Hill, and dust themselves along the verge of the brick-walk.

[John] Ray remarks that birds of the *gallinae* order, as cocks and hens, partridges and pheasants, etc., are pulveratrices such as dust themselves, using that method of cleansing their feathers and ridding themselves of their vermin. As far as I can observe, many birds that dust themselves never wash: and I once thought that those birds that wash themselves would never dust; but here I find myself mistaken; for common house-sparrows are great pulveratrices, being frequently seen grovelling and wallowing in dusty roads; and yet they are great washers. Does not the skylark dust?

June 16

Phallus impudicus, a stink-pot, comes up in Mr. Burbey's asparagus-bed.

My garden in nice order, and full of flower in bloom. Lilies, roses, fraxinellas, red valerians, irises, etc., etc., now make a gaudy show.

June 17

The nights are very hot.

The *blattae* [cockroaches] are almost subdued by the persevering assiduity of Mrs. John White, who [has] waged war on them for many months and destroyed thousands.

June 18

A cat gets down the pots of a neighbour's chimney after swallows' nests.

Received an hogshead of port from Southampton between Mr. Yalden and myself.

June 19

Hot dry weather with an high glass. Cut my grass: four mowers cut the great mead, the slip and the shrubbery by dinner-time.

Muscae domesticae [house-flies] swarm in every room . . . They are destroyed by a poisonous water called fly-water, set in basins; and by bird-lime twigs laid across pans of water.

June 20

The smoke from lime-kilns hangs along the forest in level tracks for miles.

My favourite old Galloway, who is touched in his wind, was allowed to taste no water for 21 days; by which means his infirmity grew much less troublesome. He was turned to grass every night and became fat and hearty, and moved with ease. During this abstinence he staled less than usual, and his dung was harder and drier than what usually falls from grass-horses. After refraining awhile he showed little propensity for drink. A good lesson this to people, who by perpetual guzzling create a perpetual thirst. When permitted to drink he showed no eagerness for water.

June 21

Ricked up my hay without one drop of rain; though the clouds, a sinking glass and a hollow wind threatened very hard.

Discovered a curious orchis in the hollow shady part of Newton Lane, just beyond the cross. It is the *orchis alba bifolia minor calcari oblongo* [lesser butterfly orchid]; grew with a very long stem, and has been in flower some weeks. I brought away the flower, and marked the root, intending to transplant it into the garden, when the leaves are withered.

June 22

Hollyhocks, sweet-Williams, nasturtiums and everlasting peas blossom.

The rats have carried away six out of seven of my biggest Bantam chickens; some from the stable, and some from the brew-house.

Swallows are hawking after food for their young till near nine o' clock.

All summer long is the swallow a most instructive pattern of unwearied industry and affection; for, from morning to night, while there is a family to be supported, she spends the whole day in skimming close to the ground, and exerting the most sudden turns and quick evolutions. Avenues, and long walks under hedges, and pasture fields, and mown meadows where cattle graze, are her delight, especially if there are trees interspersed; because in such spots insects most abound. When a fly is taken a smart snap from her bill is heard, resembling the noise at the shutting of a watch-case; but the motion of the mandibles are too quick for the eye . . . Horsemen on wide downs are often closely attended by a little party of swallows for miles together, which plays before and behind them, sweeping around, and collecting all skulking insects that are roused by the trampling of the horses' feet: when the wind blows hard, without this expedient, they are often forced to settle to pick up their lurking prey.

June 23

The dwarf upright larkspurs make a fine show.

June 24

I [have] procured a litter of four or five young hedgehogs which appeared to be about five days old. They, I find, like puppies, are born blind and could not see when they came to

my hands. No doubt their spines are soft and flexible at the time of their birth, or else the poor dam would have but a bad time of it in the critical moment of parturition. But it is plain that they soon harden, for these little pigs had such stiff prickles on their backs and sides as would easily have fetched blood had they not been handled with caution. Their spines are quite white at this age; and they have little hanging ears, which I do not remember to be discernible in the old ones. They can, in part, at this age draw their skin down over their faces; but are not able to contract themselves into a ball as they do, for the sake of defence, when full grown.

June 25

Young fawns in the Holt.

Cherries begin to come in; artichokes for supper. Cauliflowers, cos lettuce, marrowfat peas, carrots, summer cabbage and small beans in great profusion and perfection.

Tried for rats over the stable and brew-house with a ferret, but did not succeed.

June 26

Many children continue to die of the measles, among the rest the youngest of Mrs. Hale's this morning; and the whooping-cough rather gets worse than better.

June 27

Met a cart of whortleberries on the road.

Hung the net over the cherry-trees at the end of the house to keep off the magpies, which come to our very windows between three and four in the morning. The daws also from the church have invaded my neighbours' cherries. Pies and daws are very impudent!

June 28

Foxgloves, thistles, butterfly-orchis blow in the High Wood.

June 29

Some swallows this day bring out their broods.

The progressive method by which the young are introduced into life is very amusing: first, they emerge from the shaft with difficulty enough, and often fall down into the rooms below. For a day or so they are fed on the chimney-top, and then are

conducted to the dead leafless bough of some tree, where, sitting in a row, they are attended with great assiduity, and may then be called perchers. In a day or two more they become flyers, but are still unable to take their own food; therefore they play about near the place where the dams are hawking for flies; and when a mouthful is collected, at a certain signal given, the dam and nestling advance, rising towards each other, and meeting at an angle; the young one all the while uttering . . . a little note of gratitude and complacency.

June 30

Green peas soup every day.

JULY

July 1

As I was visiting last Tuesday at Bramshott I saw on the Portsmouth road Burgoyne's light-horse marching down to embark for North America. The horses were fine, and the men fine young fellows; but they all looked very grave, and did not seem much to admire their destination. The Atlantic is no small frith for cavalry to be transported over. The expense will be enormous!

July 2

We put Timothy into a tub of water, and found that he sank gradually, and walked on the bottom of the tub; he seemed quite out of his element and was much dismayed. This species seems not at all amphibious.

July 3

Thatched the hayricks.

July 4

Frogs migrate from ponds.

On this day my godson Littleton Etty discovered a young cuckoo in one of the yew hedges of the vicarage garden, sitting in a small nest that would scarce contain the bird, though not half-grown. By watching in the morning we found that the owners of the nest were hedge-sparrows, who were much busied in feeding their great booby. The nest is in so secret a place that it is to be wondered how the parent cuckoo could discover it.

July 5

I again untiled part of a roof over the nest of a swift . . . . The squab young we brought down and placed on the grass-plot, where they tumbled about, and were as helpless as a newborn child. While we contemplated their naked bodies, their unwieldy disproportioned *abdomina*, and their heads, too heavy for their necks to support, we could not but wonder when we reflected that these shiftless beings in a little more than a fortnight would be able to dash through the air almost with the inconceivable swiftness of a meteor; and perhaps, in their emigration must traverse vast continents and oceans as distant as the equator.

July 6

Mrs. Eveleigh says that the churring of the fern-owl [nightjar] is like the noise of a razor-grinder's wheel.

This bird is most punctual in beginning its song exactly at the close of day; so exactly that I have known it strike up more than once or twice just at the report of the Portsmouth evening gun, which we can hear when the weather is still.

Paid Will Dewey for eight dozen of young sparrows.

July 7

A pair of sparrow-hawks [have] bred in a crow's nest in the

Hanger. A boy climbed the tree and found the young so fledge that they all escaped. But he brought down a young blackbird, a young house-martin and jay, clean-picked and half-devoured, which the dams had carried to their brood. The old ones have made havoc for some days among the young swallows and martins, which being but just out have no powers or command of wing. They carried off also from a farm-yard a young duck larger than themselves.

The swallow, probably the male bird, is the *excubitor* to house-martins and other little birds, announcing the approach of birds of prey. For as soon as an hawk appears, with a shrill alarming note he calls all the swallows and martins about him; who pursue in a body, and buffet and strike their enemy till they have driven him from the village, darting down from above on his back, and rising in a perpendicular line in perfect security. This bird will also sound the alarm, and strike at cats when they climb on the roofs of houses, or otherwise approach the nests.

July 8

When we came to Evely Corner, a hen partridge came out of a ditch and ran along shivering with her wings and crying out as if wounded, and unable to get from us. While the dam acted this distress, the boy who attended me saw her brood, that was small and unable to fly, run for shelter into an old fox-earth under the bank.

The more I reflect on the affection of animals, the more I am astonished at its effects. Nor is the violence of this affection more wonderful than the shortness of its duration. Thus every hen is in her turn the virago of the yard in proportion to the helplessness of her brood; and will fly in the face of a dog or a sow in defence of those chickens, which in a few weeks she will drive before her with relentless cruelty.

July 9

Bunches of snakes' eggs are found under some straw near the hotbeds.

Cranberries are offered at the door.

July 10

The young cuckoo gets fledge and grows bigger than its nest. It is very fierce and pugnacious.

July 11

Dark and sultry, much lightning. The heat overcomes the grass-mowers and makes them sick.

There is a sort of wild-bee [carder bee] frequenting the garden-campion for the sake of its tomentum, which probably it turns to some purpose in the business of nidification. It is very pleasant to see with what address it strips off the pubes, running from the top to the bottom of a branch, and shaving it bare with all the dexterity of an hoop-shaver. When it has got a vast bundle almost as large as itself, it flies away, holding it secure between its chin and its forelegs.

July 12

Young pheasants.

July 13

Farmer Knight, having ploughed Baker's Hill twice before, stirred it across today. The weeds are all killed, and the soil is baked as hard as stone; and is as rough as the sea in an hard gale. The clods stand on end as high as one's knees.

Wheat begins to turn colour. It is very large and tall, and will have a great burden of straw.

Bestowed great waterings in the garden.

July 14

Kine, whether oxen, cows, calves or heifers, retire constantly to the water during the hotter hours; where, being more exempt from flies, and inhaling the coolness of that element, some belly-deep, and some only to mid-leg, they ruminate and solace themselves from about 10 in the morning till four in the afternoon, and then return to their feeding. During this great proportion of the day they drop much dung, in which insects nestle; and so supply food for the fish, which would be poorly subsisted but for this contingency. Thus nature, who is a great economist, converts the recreation of one animal to the support of another!

July 15

The cat gets up on the roof of the house and catches young bats as they come forth behind the sheet of lead at the bottom of the chimney.

July 16

The china-pinks that stood the winter blow beautifully. Scarlet martagons blossom.

July 17

The jasmine is so sweet that I am obliged to quit my chamber.

July 18

Swifts dash and frolic about, and seem to be teaching their young the use of their wings.

Farmers complain their wheat is blighted.

July 19

Young pheasants fly.

Oaks put out their midsummer shoots, some of which are red, and some yellow; and those oaks that were stripped by caterpillars begin to be clothed with verdure. Many beeches are loaded with mast, so that their boughs become very pendulous and look brown.

July 20

The white owl has young. It brings a mouse to its nest about every five minutes, beginning at sunset.

We have had, ever since I can remember, a pair of white owls that constantly breed under the eaves of this church . . . . About an hour before sunset (for then the mice begin to run) they sally forth in quest of prey, and hunt all round the hedges of meadows and small enclosures for them, which seem to be their only food. In this irregular country we can stand on an eminence and see them beat the fields over like a setting-dog, and often drop down in the grass or corn. I have minuted these birds with my watch for an hour together, and have found that they return to their nests, the one or the other of them, about once in five minutes . . . As they take their prey with their claws, so they carry it in their claws to their nest. But, as the feet are necessary in their ascent under the tiles, they constantly perch first on the roof of the chancel, and shift the mouse from their claws to their bill, that the feet may be at liberty to take hold of the plate on the wall as they are rising under the eaves.

White owls seem not (but in this I am not positive) to hoot at all: all that clamorous hooting appears to me to come from the wood kinds. The white owl does indeed snore and hiss in a tremendous manner; and these menaces will answer the intention of intimidating: for I have known a whole village up in arms on such an occasion, imagining the churchyard to be full of goblins and spectres. White owls also often scream horribly as they fly along; from this screaming probably arose the common people's imaginary species of screech-owl, which they superstitiously think attends the windows of dying persons.

July 21

The garden is much refreshed by showers.

Bees, when a shower approaches, hurry home.

July 22

Made black-currant jelly and raspberry jam.

July 23

Those maggots that make worm-holes in tables, chairs, bedposts, etc., and destroy wooden furniture, especially where there is any sap, are the larvae of the *plinus pectinicornis*. This insect, it is probable, deposits its eggs on the surface and the worms eat their way in. In their holes they turn into their pupa state, and so come forth winged in July, eating their way through the valences or curtains of a bed, or any other furniture that happens to obstruct their passage. They seem to be most inclined to breed in beech: hence beech will not make lasting utensils or furniture.

July 24

Puff-balls come up in my grass-plot and walks: they came from the common in the turf. There are many fairy-rings in my walks; in these the puff-balls thrive best. The fairy-rings alter and vary in their shape.

July 25

Lime-trees are fragrant: the golden tassels are beautiful. Dr. Chandler tells us that in the south of France an infusion of the blossoms of the lime-tree, *tilia*, is in much esteem as a remedy for coughs, hoarsenesses, fevers, etc., and that at Nîmes he saw an avenue of limes that was quite ravaged and torn to pieces by people greedily gathering the bloom, which they dried and kept for their purposes. Upon the strength of this information we made some tea of lime-blossoms, and found it a very soft, well-flavoured, pleasant saccharine julep, in taste much resembling the juice of liquorice.

July 26

By observing two glow-worms which were brought from the field to the bank in the garden, it appeared to us that those little creatures put out their lamps between 11 and 12, and shine no more for the rest of the night.

July 27

This morning, in a basket, I packed a little earthen pot full of wet moss, and in it some sticklebacks, male and female; the females big with spawn: some lamperns; some bullheads; but I

could produce no minnows. This basket will be in Fleet Street by eight this evening; so I hope [Peter] Mazell will have them fresh and fair tomorrow morning. I gave some directions, in a letter, to what particulars the engraver should be attentive.

July 28

Children gather strawberries every morning from the Hanger where the tall beeches were felled.

Where old beech-trees are cleared away, the naked ground in a year or two becomes covered with strawberry plants, the seeds of which must have lain in the ground for an age at least.

July 29

Men hoe turnips.

The beetles begin to hum about at the close of day.

July 30

Peacocks begin to moult, and cast their splendid train.

Happening to make a visit to my neighbour's peacocks, I could not help observing that the trains of those magnificent birds appear by no means to be their tails; those long feathers growing not from their *uropygium* [rump], but all up their backs. A range of short, brown, stiff feathers, about six inches long, fixed in the *uropygium*, is the real tail, and serves as the fulcrum to prop the train, which is long and top-heavy when set on end. When the train is up, nothing appears of the bird before but its head and neck; but this would not be the case were those long feathers fixed only in the rump, as may be seen by the turkey-cock when in a strutting attitude. By a strong muscular vibration these birds can make the shafts of their long feathers clatter like the swords of a sword-dancer; they then trample very quick with their feet, and run backwards towards the females.

July 31

The ground dried to powder.
   Horses at plough so teased by flies as to be quite frantic.

AUGUST

August 1

Clouds of dust attend the drags and harrows.

About half-hour after three in the afternoon the people of Selborne were surprised by a shower of aphids which fell in these parts. I was not at home; but those that were walking the street at that juncture found themselves covered with these insects, which settled also on the trees and gardens, and blackened all the vegetables where they alighted. My annuals were covered with them; and some onions were quite coated over with them . . . These armies, no doubt, were then in a state of emigration, and shifting their quarters; and might [have] come, as far as we know, from the great hop plantations of Kent or Sussex, the wind being that day at east.

August 2

People gather mushrooms.

August 3

Sowed a crop of prickly-seeded spinach to stand the winter: the ground was very hard and cloddy and would not rake; so we levelled it down as well as we could with a garden-roller and sprinkled it over with fine dusty mould to cover the seeds.

August 4

Bottled off the hogshead of port between Mr. Yalden and myself.

We surprised a large viper, which seemed very heavy and bloated, as it lay in the grass basking in the sun. When we came to cut it up, we found that the abdomen was crowded with young, 15 in number; the shortest of which measured full seven inches, and were about the size of full-grown earth-worms. This little fry issued into the world with the true viper spirit about them, showing great alertness as soon as disengaged from the belly of the dam: they twisted and wriggled about, and set themselves up, and gaped very wide when touched with a stick, showing manifest tokens of menace and defiance, though as yet they had no manner of fangs that we could find, even with the help of our glasses.

August 5

My pendant pantry, made of deal and fine fly-wire, and suspended in the great walnut-tree, proves an incomparable preservative for meat against flesh-flies. The flesh by hanging in a brisk current of air becomes dry on the surface, and keeps till it is tender without tainting.

August 6

Large bat appears

The summer through I have seen but two of that large species of bat which I call *vespertilio altivolans* [noctule bat], from its manner of feeding in the air . . . . In the extent of their wings they measured 14 inches and an half, and four inches and an half from the nose to the tip of the tail; their heads were large, their nostrils bilobated, their shoulders broad and muscular, and their whole bodies fleshy and plump. Nothing could be more sleek and soft than their fur, which was of a bright chestnut colour; their maws were full of food, but so macerated that the quality could not be distinguished; their livers, kidneys and hearts were large, and their bowels covered with fat. They weighed each, when entire, full one ounce and one drachm . . . . These creatures send forth a very rancid and offensive smell.

August 7

The kingfisher darts along like an arrow.

A good ornithologist should be able to distinguish birds by their air as well as by their colours and shape . . . For, though it must not be said that every species of bird has a manner peculiar to itself, yet there is somewhat in most genera at least, that at first sight discriminates them . . . Thus kites and buzzards sail round in circles with wings expanded and motionless . . . The kestrel, or wind-hover, has a peculiar mode of hanging in the air in one place, his wings all the while being briskly agitated. Hen-harriers fly low over heaths or fields of corn, and beat the ground regularly like a pointer or setting-dog. Owls move in a buoyant manner, as if lighter than air; they seem to want ballast . . . . Magpies and jays flutter with powerless wings, and make no dispatch; herons seem encumbered with too much sail for their light bodies; but these vast hollow wings are necessary in carrying burdens, such as large fishes, and the like . . . starlings as it were swim along, while missel-thrushes use a wild and desultory flight . . . Skylarks rise and fall perpendicularly as they sing: woodlarks hang poised in the air; and titlarks rise and fall in large curves, singing in their descent.

August 8

We have shot 31 blackbirds and saved our gooseberries.

The honey-bees suck the gooseberries where the birds have broke the skin.

August 9

Thorough hot weather.

Wheat-harvest begins with us.

August 10

A labourer has mown out in the precincts of Hartley Wood, during the course of this summer, as many pheasants' nests as contained 60 eggs!

August 11

Put the bulbous roots in paper-bags, and hung them in the lumber-garret. They are vastly increased, especially the hyacinths.

August 12

Men bind their wheat all day. The harvesters complain of the heat.

August 13

Some martins, dispossessed of their nests by sparrows, return to them again when their enemies are shot.

Many annuals are shrivelled up for want of moisture.

August 14

Harvest-bugs bite the ladies.

Farmer Spencer's charcoal-making in his orchard almost suffocated us. The poisonous smoke penetrated into our parlour, and bedchambers, and was very offensive in the night.

August 15

On this day at 10 in the morning some sober and intelligent people felt at Noar Hill what they thought to be a slight shock of an earthquake. A mother and her son perceived the house to tremble at the same time while one was above stairs and the other below; and each called to the other to know what was the matter. A young man in the field near heard a strange rumbling.

August 16

Sun, sweet harvest weather. Much wheat housed.

Gleaners carry home large loads.

August 17

The flea[-beetle] eats up the young turnips at a vast rate.

In very hot summers they abound to an amazing degree, and, as you walk in a field or in a garden, make a pattering like rain, by jumping on the leaves of the turnips or cabbages.

August 18

Harvest scenes are now very beautiful!
  Swans flounce and dive.

August 19

Mrs. Barker, and her daughters Mary and Elizabeth, and Mrs.
Chandler, and her infant daughter, and nursemaid, went all in
a cart to see the great oak in the Holt, which is deemed by Mr.
Marsham of Stratton in Norfolk to be the biggest in this island.
Brother Thomas and Dr. Chandler rode on horseback. They
all dined under the shade of this tree.

August 20

On this day Farmer Spencer built a large wheat-rick near his
house, the contents of which all came from a field near
Westcroft Barn at the full distance of a mile. Five waggons were
going all day.
  Many creatures are endowed with a ready discernment to
see what will turn to their own advantage and emolument . . .
[thus] poultry watch for waggons loaded with wheat, and
running after them pick up a number of grains which are
shaken from the sheaves by the agitation of the carriages.

August 21

Boiled up some apricots with sugar to preserve them.

August 22

Caught about 100 wasps in the fallen codlins, which were
gnawn and scooped hollow.
  Wild ragwort, scabious, hawkweed, knapweed, burdock,
yarrow, restharrow, etc., in flower.

August 23

Though white butterflies abound, and lay many eggs on the cabbages; yet through over-heat and want of moisture they do not hatch and turn to palmers; but dry and shrivel to nothing.

August 24

The vine Murdoch Middleton [nursery-man] sent for Warner's Black Hamburg seems, as it approaches towards ripening, to be some ordinary sort of white grape.

Scarce any of Murdoch Middleton's trees turn out the sorts sent for.

August 25

My great apricot-tree appeared in the morning to have been robbed of some of its ripe fruit by a dog that had stood up on his hind legs and eaten off some of the lower apricots, several of which were gnawn and left on the ground with some shoots of the tree. On the border were many fresh prints of a dog's feet. I have known a dog eat ripe gooseberries as they hung on the trees.

August 26

Timothy the tortoise, who has spent the two last months amidst the umbrageous forests of the asparagus-beds, begins now to be sensible of the chilly autumnal mornings; and therefore suns himself under the laurel hedge, into which he retires at night. He is become sluggish, and does not seem to take any food.

August 27

Gathered my first figs.

A fern-owl this evening showed off in a very unusual and entertaining manner by hawking round and round the circumference of my great spreading oak for 20 times following, keeping mostly close to the grass, but occasionally glancing up amidst the boughs of the tree. This amusing bird was then in pursuit of a brood of some particular *phalaena* belonging to the oak, of which there are several sorts; and exhibited on the occasion a command of wing superior, I think, to that of the swallow itself . . . . These peculiar birds can only be watched and observed for two hours in the twenty-four; and then in a dubious twilight, an hour after sunset, and an hour before sunrise.

August 28

The air is full of thistle-down blown from the top of the Hanger.

August 29

Gathered the first plate of peaches.

The hornets, though few in number, make havoc among the nectarines.

August 30

Hop-picking becomes general. The women earn good wages this year; some of them pick 24 bushels in a day, at three halfpence per bushel.

August 31

Farmer Spencer's wheat-rick, when it was near finished, parted and fell down.

The poor steal the farmers' corn by night. The losers offer rewards, but in vain.

SEPTEMBER

September 1

The young martins of the second flight peep out of their nests.

September 2

Wrynecks, birds so called, appear on the grass-plots and walks. They walk a little as well as hop, and thrust their bills into the turf in quest, I conclude, of ants, which are their food. While they hold their bills in the grass they draw out their prey with their tongues, which are so long as to be coiled round their heads.

September 3

When the boys bring me wasps' nests, my bantam fowls fare deliciously; and when the combs are pulled to pieces, devour the young wasps in their maggot state with the highest glee and delight. Any insect-eating bird would do the same, and therefore I have often wondered that the accurate Mr. Ray should call one species of buzzard *Buteo apivoros, sive vespivorus*, or the honey-buzzard, because some combs of wasps happened to be found in one of their nests. The combs were conveyed thither doubtless for the sake of the maggots or nymphs, and not for their honey; since none is to be found in the combs of wasps. Birds of prey occasionally feed on insects: Thus have I seen a tame kite picking up the female ants, full of eggs, with much satisfaction.

September 4

The great heats are now abated, and the dust is laid.

Lady's tresses blow, and abound in the Long Lythe. A rare plant.

September 5

I saw lately a small ichneumon-fly attack a spider much larger than itself on the grass-walk. When the spider made any resistance the ichneumon applied her tail to him and stung him with great vehemence, so that he soon became dead and motionless. The ichneumon then running backward drew her prey very nimbly over the walk into the standing grass. This spider would be deposited in some hole where the ichneumon would lay some eggs; and as soon as the eggs were hatched the carcase would afford ready food for the maggots.

September 6

Wheatears (birds) continue to be taken: [they] are esteemed an elegant dish.

At the time of wheat-harvest [these birds] begin to be taken in great numbers; are sent for sale in vast quantities to Brighton and Tonbridge; and appear at the tables of all the gentry that entertain with any degree of elegance.

September 7

Swallows and house-martins dip much in ponds.

Each species of *hirundo* drinks as it flies along, sipping the surface of the water; but the swallow alone, in general, washes on the wing, by dropping into a pool for many times together.

September 8

The wasps (which are without number this dry, hot summer) attack the grapes in a grievous manner. Hung up 16 bottles with treacle and beer, which make great havoc among them. Bagged about 50 of the best bunches in crêpe bags.

September 9

Beautiful autumnal weather . . . On the steep chalky end of Wheatham Hill I discovered a large plant of the deadly-nightshade (*belladonna*) full of ripe fruit, and on the bogs of Bin's Pond in Woolmer Forest the same day that peculiar plant the sun-dew (*rorella*) in plenty. There are, it seems, on the same bog plenty of cranberry plants, but I could not venture on the moss to look after them . . . . I thought I discovered a small *parnassia* [grass-of-parnassus], but was not sure. Found also southernwood (*abrotanum*) in a lane; and dyer's-weed [dyer's greenweed] (*luteola*), very vigorous and full of seed, in a farmyard at Farringdon.

The standing objection to botany has always been, that it is a pursuit that amuses the fancy and exercises the memory, without improving the mind or advancing any real knowledge: and where the science is carried no farther than a mere systematic classification, the charge is but too true. But the

botanist that is desirous of wiping off this aspersion should be by no means content with a list of names; he should study plants philosophically, should investigate the laws of vegetation, should examine the powers and virtues of efficacious herbs, should promote their cultivation; and graft the gardener, the planter and the husbandman, on the phytologist . . . . Instead of examining the minute distinctions of every species of each obscure genus, the botanist should endeavour to make himself acquainted with those that are useful. You shall see a man readily ascertain every herb of the field, yet hardly know wheat from barley, or at least one sort of wheat or barley from another. But of all sorts of vegetation the grasses seem to be most neglected; neither the farmer nor the grazier seem to distinguish the annual from the perennial, the hardy from the tender, nor the succulent and nutritive from the dry and juiceless. The study of grasses would be of great consequence to a northerly and grazing kingdom. The botanist that could improve the sward of the district where he lived would be an useful member of society; to raise a thick turf on a naked soil would be worth volumes of systematic knowledge.

September 10

Hedgehogs bore holes in the grass-walks to come at the plantain roots, which they eat upwards.

Redbreasts feed on elder-berries, enter rooms, and spoil the furniture.

September 11

Gathered the first mulberry that my tree ever produced: it was very sweet; and good, but small. There are some more on the tree.

Harvest-moon.

September 12

The congregating flocks of hirundines on the church and tower are very beautiful and amusing! When they fly off altogether from the roof, on any alarm, they quite swarm in the air. But they soon settle in heaps, and preening their feathers, and lifting up their wings to admit the sun, seem highly to enjoy the warm situation. Thus they spend the heat of the day preparing for their emigration and, as it were, consulting when and where they are to go.

September 13

Collected mushroom spawn and laid it up to dry.

September 14

We found in a field near a hedge the slough of a large snake, which seemed to have been newly-cast. From circumstances it appeared as turned wrong-side outward, and as drawn off backward, like a stocking or woman's glove. Not only the whole skin, but scales from the very eyes are peeled off, and appear in the head of the slough like a pair of spectacles. The

reptile, at the time of changing his coat, had entangled himself intricately in the grass and weeds, so that the friction of the stalks and blades might promote this curious shifting of his *exuviae* . . . As the convexity of the scales of the eyes in the slough are/is now inward, that circumstance alone is a proof that the skin has been turned: not to mention that now the present inside is much darker than the outer. If you look through the scales of the snake's eyes from the concave side, viz.: as the reptile used them, they lessen objects much. Thus it appears, from what has been said, that snakes crawl out of the mouth of their own sloughs, and quit the tail part last; just as eels are skinned by a cookmaid.

September 15

Black, warty water-efts [newts] with fin-tails and yellow bellies are drawn up in the well-bucket.

Gathered many of the baking pears to disburden the boughs, and keep them from breaking.

September 16

When we call loudly through the speaking-trumpet to Timothy, he does not seem to regard the noise.

September 17

The sky this evening being what they call a mackerel-sky, was most beautiful, and much admired in many parts of the country. Italian skies!

September 18

Gathered some nonpareils and golden rennets, which are very fair and ready to be laid up, being a fortnight at least earlier than common.

September 19

Much gossamer on the grass, and floating in the air.

Strange and superstitious as the notions about [these cobweb-like appearances] were formerly, nobody in these days doubts but that they are the real production of small spiders, which swarm in the fields in fine weather in autumn, and have a power of shooting out webs from their tails so as to render themselves buoyant, and lighter than air.

September 20

Last week Mrs. Burbey had a respectable farmer, a cousin, with her on a visit. This person waked in the night, and found himself standing naked in the cartway with his nightcap in his hand. How he came there he could not imagine: but there was just light enough for him to see that the sash of his chamber was up; and therefore he concluded he must have come down from thence. Finding the doors all locked he was forced to call up the family, who were astonished to see their visitor in his shirt, and much confused and frightened. The poor man received a cut on the sole of one of his feet, and a small contusion on one knee: and this was all the harm that he received from descending, fast asleep, for the space of 12 feet and a half, down on the bare pavement.

September 21

Tops of the beeches, *fagi*, are tinged with yellow.

The whole air of the village of an evening is perfumed by effluvia from the hops drying in the kilns.

September 22

This morning the swallows rendezvoused in a neighbour's walnut-tree. At the dawn of the day they arose altogether in infinite numbers, occasioning such a rushing with the strokes of their wings as might be heard to a considerable distance. Since that no flock has appeared, only some late broods, and stragglers.

September 23

Black snails [slugs] lie out, and copulate. Vast swagging clouds.

My Bantam chickens, which have been kept in the scullery every night till now for fear of rats, that carried away the first brood from the brew-house, went up last week to the beam above the stable. The earnest and early propensity of the *gallinae* to roost on high is very observable, and discovers a strong dread impressed on their spirits respecting vermin that may annoy them on the ground during the hours of darkness. Hence poultry, if left to themselves and not housed, will perch, the winter through, on yew-trees and fir-trees; and turkeys and guinea-fowls, heavy as they are, get up into apple-trees; pheasants also in woods sleep on trees to avoid foxes: while pea-fowls climb to the tops of the tallest trees round their owner's house for security, let the weather be ever so cold or blowing. Partridges, it is true, roost on the ground, not having the faculty of perching; but then the same fear prevails in their minds: for through apprehensions from polecats, weasels and stoats, they never trust themselves to coverts, but nestle together in the midst of large fields, far removed from hedges and coppices, which they love to frequent/haunt in the day;

and where at that season they can skulk more secure from the ravages of rapacious birds. As to ducks and geese, their awkward, splay, web-feet forbid them to settle on trees: they therefore, in the hours of darkness and danger, betake themselves to their own element, the water, where, amidst large lakes and pools, like ships riding at anchor, they float the whole night long in peace and security.

September 24

The leaves of the Virginia creeper turn of a blood colour.

September 25

Much barley housed this day.

The Michaelmas daisies covered with butterflies and other gaudy insects make a very gallant appearance in the sunshine.

September 26

Began to light fires in the parlour.

September 27

Showers, stormy day. Gardens are torn to pieces, and great boughs off trees.

Put nine hyacinths to blow in the glasses over the chimney [-piece].

September 28

Made 18 quarts of elder-juice, and put to it 36 pounds of 4½ sugar, which made 29 quarts of syrup. Memo.: two gallons and half of picked berries, moderately squeezed, produced about a gallon of juice.

September 29

Herrings come into season.

I managed to get a sight of the female moose belonging to the Duke of Richmond at Goodwood; but was greatly disappointed, when I arrived at the spot, to find that it had died . . . I found it in an old greenhouse, slung under the belly and chin by ropes, and in a standing posture; but, though it had been dead for so short a time, it was in so putrid a state that the stench was hardly supportable . . . . From the fore-feet to the belly behind the shoulder it measured three feet and eight inches: the length of the legs before and behind consisted a great deal in the *tibia*, which was strangely long; but in my haste to get out of the stench, I forgot to measure that joint exactly.

September 30

The men are weeding the garden, which is very much overrun with groundsel.

OCTOBER

October 1

Cleaned my well by drawing out about 100 buckets of muddy water . . . Nothing had been done to this well for about 40 years. The man at the bottom in the cleaning brought up several marbles and taws that we had thrown down when children.

Deep and tremendous as is the well at Heards, John Gillman, an idiot, fell on the bottom of it twice in one morning; and was taken out alive, and survived the strange accident for many years.

October 2

The quantity of potatoes planted in this parish was very great, and the produce, on ground unused to that root, prodigious. David Long had 200 bushels on half an acre.

October 3

The cat frolics, and plays with the falling leaves.

One of the first trees that becomes naked is the walnut; the mulberry, and the ash especially if it bears many keys, and the horse-chestnut come next. All lopped trees, while their heads are young, carry their leaves a long while. Apple-trees and peaches remain green till very late, often till the end of November. Young beeches never cast their leaves till spring, till the new leaves sprout and push them off . . . . Tall beeches cast their leaves towards the end of October.

October 4

This day has been at Selborne the honey-market: for a person from Chert came over with a cart, to whom all the villages round brought their hives and sold their contents. This year has proved a good one to the upland bee-gardens, but not to those near the forest.

October 5

Crossbills, *loxiae curvirostrae*, among Mrs. Snooke's Scotch pines.

October 6

A vast flock of ravens over the Hanger: more than 60!

Ravens in their common mode of flying have a peculiarity attending them not unworthy of notice: they turn over in the air quite on their backs, and that not now and then, but frequently; often every two or three hundred yards. When this odd attitude betides them they fall down several fathoms, uttering a loud crow, and then right themselves again . . . . Ravens spend their leisure time over some hanging-wood in a sort of mock fight, dashing and diving at each other continually; while their loud croakings make the woody steeps re-echo again.

October 7

Deep autumnal darkness.

Rooks carry off the walnuts from my trees.

October 8

Bought of bright hops 21 pounds; of brown 49.

October 9

Nuts fall very fast from the hedges.

October 10

Flies of many sorts swarm on the bloom of ivy.

In the decline of the year, when the mornings and evenings become chilly, many species of flies (*muscae*) retire into houses and swarm in the windows. At first they are very brisk and alert: but as they grow more torpid one cannot help observing that they move with difficulty, and are scarce able to lift their legs, which seem as if glued to the glass: and by degrees many do actually stick on till they die in the place. Now as flies have flat skinny palms or soles to their feet, which enable them to walk on glass and other smooth bodies by means of the pressure of the atmosphere; may not this pressure be the means of their embarrassment as they grow more feeble: till at last their powers become quite inadequate to the weight of the incumbent air bearing hard on their more languid feet; and so at last they stick to the walls and windows, where they remain, and are found dead.

October 11

Found the *sphinx atropos*, or death's-head moth, a noble insect of a vast size. It lays its eggs on the jasmine. When handled it makes a little stridulous noise.

October 12

The hanging beech-woods begin to be beautifully tinged and to afford most lovely scapes, very engaging to the eye and imagination . . . . These scenes are worthy [of] the pencil of a Rubens.

October 13

Stormy winds, and gluts of rain.

October 14

The hop-planters of this parish returned from Weyhill Fair with cheerful faces and full purses, having sold a large crop of hops for a good price. The hops of Kent were blown away by the storms after the crop of this country was gathered in.

Two hop-waggons return with loads of woollen rags, to be spread and dug in as manure for the hop-gardens.

October 15

Transplanted six geraniums into six penny-pots to stand the winter.

Hunter's-moon.

October 16

The redbreast's note is very sweet and pleasing, did it not carry with it ugly associations of ideas and put us in mind of the approach of winter.

October 17

Gathered in the barberries, a great crop.

October 18

Gathered a plate of grapes; they are just eatable.

October 19

From the fineness of the weather, and the steadiness of the wind to the north-east I began to be possessed with a notion last Friday that we should see Mr. Blanchard in his balloon . . . At twenty minutes before three there was a cry in the street that the balloon was come. We ran into the orchard, where we found 20 or 30 neighbours assembled; and from the green bank at the south-west end of my house saw a dark blue speck at a most prodigious height, dropping as it were from the sky, and hanging amidst the regions of the upper air, between the weather-cock of the tower and the top of the maypole. At first, coming towards us, it did not seem to make any way; but we soon discovered that its velocity was very considerable. For in a few minutes it was over the maypole; and then over the fox on

my great parlour chimney; and in 10 minutes more behind my great walnut-tree. The machine looked mostly of a dark blue colour; but sometimes reflected the rays of the sun, and appeared of a bright yellow. With a telescope I could discern the boat, and the ropes that supported it. To my eye this vast balloon appeared no bigger than a large tea-urn.

October 20

Acorns abound; the hogs in the lanes and woods seem to be half-fat.

October 21

The Holybourne truffler finds encouragement in our woods and hangers as he frequently passes along the village. He is a surly fellow, and not communicative. He is attended by two little cur-dogs, which he leads in a string.

October 22

Miserable, cold rains.

October 23

Redwings on our common.
Much peat carted through the village.

October 24

I planted my bulbs; a row of hyacinths, above 60, and a few tulips and polyanth narcissus on the edge of the fruit-border; a row of tulips and polyanth narcissus, corn-flags and jonquils next Parson's; and two rows of crocus under the buttery window.

October 25

Planted a large layer of musk-rose from Mr. Budd against the boards of the old barn.

October 26

Two of my brother Henry's goldfish have been sick and cannot live with the rest in the glass bowl: but in a tin bucket by themselves they soon become lively and vigorous.

Nothing can be more amusing than a glass bowl containing such fishes: the double refractions of the glass and water represent them, when moving, in a shifting and changeable variety of dimensions, shades and colours; while the two mediums, assisted by the concavo-convex shape of the vessel, magnify and distort them vastly . . . Some people exhibit this sort of fish in a very fanciful way; for they cause a glass bowl to be blown with a large hollow space within, that does not communicate with it. In this cavity they put a bird occasionally; so that you may see a goldfinch or a linnet hopping as it were in the midst of the water, and the fishes swimming in a circle round it.

October 27

Larks frolic much in the air. When they are in that mood the larkers catch them in nets by means of a twinkling-glass.

October 28

Many little insects, most of which seem to be *tipulae* [crane-flies], continue still to sport and play about in the air, not only when the sun shines warm, but even in fog and gentle rain, and after sunset. They appear at times the winter through in mild seasons, and even in frost and snow when the sun shines warm. They retire into trees, especially evergreens.

October 29

From the scantiness of grass I have given for some time nine pence per pound for butter, a price here not known before.

October 30

New-coped the top of my kitchen chimney, mended the tiling, and touched the inside of the roofing to keep out the drifting snow.

October 31

Many people are tied up about the head on account of tooth-aches and face-aches.

NOVEMBER

November 1

My brother's turkeys avail themselves much of the beech-mast which they find in his grove: they also delight in acorns, walnuts and hazel-nuts. No wonder therefore that they subsist wild in the woods of America, where they are supposed to be indigenous. They swallow the hazel-nuts whole.

November 2

Leaves fall very fast. My hedges show beautiful lights and shades: the yellow of the tall maples makes a fine contrast against the green hazels.

November 3

Driving rain and wind . . . . Seagulls, winter-mews, haunt the fallows.

November 4

Stewed some truffles: the flavour of their juice very fine, but the roots hard and gritty. They were boiled in water, then sliced, and stewed in gravy.

107

The *rallus porzana*, or spotted water-rail, a rare bird, was shot in the sedge of Bin's Pond . . . . I sent it to London to be stuffed and preserved. A beautiful bird.

November 5

Flying over Farringdon Heath, the first grey crow [hooded crow] that I ever saw in the district of Selborne.

The evening manoeuvres of the rooks at this season of the year are curious. Just before dusk they return in long strings from the foraging of the day, and rendezvous by thousands over Selborne Down, where they wheel round in the air, and sport and dive in a playful manner; all the while exerting their voices and making a loud cawing, which being blended and softened by the distance that we are from them becomes a confused noise, or chiding, or rather a pleasing murmur very engaging to the imagination, and not unlike the cry of a pack of hounds in hollow woods, or the rushing of the wind in tall trees, or the tide tumbling on the pebbly shore. When the ceremony is over, with the last gleam of the day they retire for the night to the deep beechen-woods of Tisted and Ropley.

November 6

Last night [at Mr. Gauler's] we had grand fire-works. Roman candles, serpents, and sky-rockets.

Gathered in all the grapes, about a bushel, the weather threatening for more frost. Spread the best bunches on a sheet in the dining-room.

November 7

A chased hind ran through the parish and was taken at Penton. She ran but two hours, the ground being too hard for her feet.

At present the deer of the Holt are much thinned and reduced by the night-hunters, who perpetually harass them in spite of the efforts of the numerous keepers, and the severe penalties that have been put in force against them as often as they have been detected, and rendered liable to the lash of the law. Neither fines nor imprisonment can deter them: so impossible is it to extinguish the spirit of sporting, which seems to be inherent in human nature.

November 8

Fog, most sweet sunshine. Infinite quantities of haws and sloes.

November 9

Magpies sometimes, I see, perch on the backs of sheep, and pick the lice and ticks out of their wool; nay mount on their very heads; while those meek quadrupeds seem pleased, and stand perfectly still, little aware that their eyes are in no small danger; and that their assiduous friends would be glad of an opportunity of picking their bones.

November 10

The wintry and huge constellation, Orion, begins now to make his appearance in the evening, exhibiting his enormous figure in the East.

November 11

The first day of winter.
    Great flocks of starlings on the downs attend the rooks.

November 12

Set the geranium pots in the garret window.

November 13

The hedge-sparrow makes its winter piping.

November 14

Thatched roofs smoke in the sun.
    Paths all mire from the frost, and thaw.

November 15

Boys play at taw on the Plestor.

November 16

Spent three hours of this day, viz., from one o'clock till four, in the midst of the downs between Andover and Winton, where we should have suffered greatly from cold and hunger had not the day proved very fine, and had not we been opposite the house of Mr. Treadgold's down farm, where we were hospitably entertained by the labourer's wife with cold spare rib, and good bread, and cheese and ale, while the driver went back to Andover to fetch a better horse. The case was, the saddle-horse, being new to his business, became jaded and restive and would not stir an inch; but was soon kept in countenance by the shaft-horse, who followed his example: so we were quite set up till four o' the clock, when another driver arrived with another lean jaded horse, and with much

difficulty assisted in dragging us to Winton, which we did not reach till six in the evening. We set out from Fyfield at 11; so we were seven hours in getting 19 miles.

November 17

Large fieldfares abound: vast clouds of them on the common.

November 18

Hogs frequent the Hanger and the High Wood, and batten on the beech-mast.

No hogs have annoyed us this year in my outlet. They usually force in after the acorns, nuts, beech and maple-mast; and occasion much trouble.

November 19

Water-cresses come in.

November 20

Ploughs are frozen out.

November 21

Made, earthed, and thatched a mushroom-bed seven feet long according to [Philip] Miller.

November 22

I sent a woman up the hill with a peck of beech-mast, which she tells me she has scattered all round the Down amidst the bushes and brakes, where there were no beeches before. I also ordered Thomas [Hoar] to sow beech-mast in the hedges all round Baker's Hill.

November 23

The downy seeds of traveller's-joy fill the air, and driving before a gale appear like insects on the wing.

My nephew Richard has been here: he was quite transported beyond himself with the pleasures of shooting; and, after walking more than 100 miles, killed *one woodcock*; which ill-fated bird took the pains to migrate from Scandinavia to be slain by a cockney, who never shot a bird before !!!

November 24

Grey, sun, sharp wind.

Trees will not subsist in sharp currents of air: thus after I had opened a vista in the hedge at the eastern corner of Baker's Hill no tree that I could plant would grow in that corner, and since I have opened a view from the bottom of the same field into the mead the ash that grew in the hedge, and now stands naked on the bastion, is dying by inches and losing all its boughs.

November 25

The miller supplies us with cold, damp flour, and says he can get no other. He adds that the best wheat is at the bottom of the mows and will not come forth till spring.

November 26

A man brought me a common seagull alive: three crows had got it down in a field, and were endeavouring to demolish it.

November 27

Timothy the tortoise sleeps in the fruit-border under the wall, covered with a hen-coop, in which is a good armful of straw. Here he will lie warm, secure and dry. His back is partly covered with mould.

When one reflects on the state of this strange being, it is a matter of wonder to find that Providence should bestow such a profusion of days, such a seeming waste of longevity, on a reptile that appears to relish it so little as to squander more than two-thirds of its existence in joyless stupor, and be lost to all sensation for months together in the profoundest of slumbers.

November 28

Hard frost . . . Children slide on the ponds.

November 29

Horses begin to lie within.

November 30

Many wild fowls haunt Woolmer Pond: in the evenings they come forth and feed on the barley-stubbles.

DECEMBER

December 1

The berries of ivy, which blowed in the end of September, now half-grown. A noble and providential supply for birds in winter and spring! For the first severe frost freezes and spoils all the haws, sometimes by the middle of November. Ivy-berries do not seem to freeze.

December 2

Vast condensations in the great parlour: the grate, the marble jambs, the tables, the chairs, the walls are covered with dew. This inconvenience may be prevented by keeping the window-shutters and door close shut in such moist seasons.

December 3

Beautiful picturesque, partial fogs along the vales, representing rivers, islands and arms of the sea! These fogs in London and some other parts were so deep that much mischief was occasioned by men falling into rivers and being overturned into ditches, etc.

Good mackerel brought to the door.

December 4

Sent two field-mice [harvest mice], a species very common in these parts (though unknown to zoologists) to Thomas Pennant Esq. of Downing in Flintshire.

From the colour, shape, size, and manner of nesting, I make no doubt that the species is nondescript. They are much smaller and more slender than the *mus domesticus medius* of Ray, and have more of the squirrel or dormouse colour: their belly is white, a straight line along their sides divides the shades of their backs and belly. They never enter into houses; are carried into ricks and barns with the sheaves; abound in harvest, and build their nests amidst the straws of the corn above the ground, and sometimes in thistles. They breed as many as eight at a litter, in a little round nest composed of the blades of grass or wheat. One of these nests I procured this autumn, most artificially platted, and composed of the blades of wheat; perfectly round, and about the size of a cricket-ball; with the aperture so ingeniously closed that there was no discovering to what part it belonged. It was so compact and well filled that it would roll across the table without being discomposed, though it contained eight little mice that were naked and blind . . . . This wonderful procreant cradle, an elegant instance of the efforts of instinct, was found in a wheat-field, suspended in the head of a thistle.

Though [these mice] hang their nests for breeding up amidst the straws of the standing corn, above the ground; yet I find that, in winter, they burrow deep in the earth, and make warm beds of grass: but their grand rendezvous seems to be in corn-ricks, into which they are carried at harvest. A neighbour housed an oat-rick lately, under the thatch of which were assembled near an hundred, most of which were taken; and some I saw. I measured them; and found that, from nose to tail they were just two inches and a quarter, and their tails just two inches long. Two of them, in a scale, weighed down just one copper halfpenny, which is about a third of an ounce avoirdupois.

December 5

Cut down and covered the artichokes: covered the rhubarb plants; and the lettuces under the fruit-wall, and the spinach lightly with straw.

Fetched some mulleins, foxgloves and dwarf laurels from the High Wood and Hanger, and planted them in the garden.

December 6

Planted out sweet-Williams, vine, and gooseberry cuttings, honeysuckle cuttings; and several crab stocks grafted from a curious and valuable green apple growing at South Lambeth in Surrey.

December 7

The wind and frost cut down the [winter] wheat, which seems to want a mantle of snow.

December 8

The Bramshott hounds kill a leash of hares [three hares] on the hill.

December 9

The trees on the Down and Hanger run in streams down their bodies.

In heavy fogs, on elevated positions especially, trees are perfect alembics [distillers]: and no one that has not attended to such matters can imagine how much water one tree will distil in a night's time by condensing the vapour, which trickles down the twigs and boughs, so as to make the ground below quite in a float. In Newton Lane . . . on a misty day, a particular oak in leaf dropped so fast that the cartway stood in puddles and the ruts ran with water, though the ground in general was dusty.

December 10

Mr. Taylor brought me a pine-apple, which was, for the season, large and well-flavoured.

December 11

Vast white frost.

December 12

One of my neighbours shot a ring-dove [wood-pigeon] . . . just as it was returning from feed and going to roost. When his wife had picked and drawn it, she found its craw stuffed with the most nice and tender tops of turnips. These she washed and boiled, and so she sat down to a choice and delicate plate of greens, culled and provided in this extraordinary manner. Hence we may see that granivorous birds, when grain fails, can subsist on the leaves of vegetables. There is reason to suppose that they would not long be healthy without: for turkeys, though corn-fed, delight in a variety of plants such as cabbage, lettuce, endive, etc., and poultry pick much grass; while geese live for months together on commons by grazing along.

December 13

Female chaffinches congregate.

For many years past I have observed that towards Christmas vast flocks of chaffinches have appeared in the fields . . . But, when I came to observe them more narrowly, I was amazed to find that they seemed to be almost all hens.

December 14

Fog, dark and spitting.

December 15

Some of my friends have sported lately in the forest: they beat the moors and morasses, and found some jack and whole snipes, most of which they killed, with a teal, a pheasant, and some partridges.

December 16

The wind is so piercing that labourers cannot stand to their work.

December 17

We have here this winter a weekly concert consisting of a first and second fiddle, two repianos, a bassoon, an haut-boy, a violin-cello, and a German-flute; to the great annoyance of the neighbouring pigs, which complain that their slumbers are interrupted, and their teeth set on edge.

December 18

Finished a paved footpath from the butcher's shop to the blacksmith's, above 70 yards. It cost just one pound.

December 19

I have received from Shields the nursery-man four peaches and nectarines, trained trees, that are to bear next year: they have fine regular heads, but are very dear!

December 20

Finished ploughing up the Ewel Close, a wheat-stubble, to prepare it for barley and grass seeds: it must be ploughed thrice. The ground is pretty dry, but tough and heavy, requiring naturally much meliorating.

December 21

The shortest day: a truly black and dismal one.
   People fall with colds.

December 22

Farmer Lassam's Dorsetshire ewes begin to lamb.

December 23

A severe tempest . . . Two men were struck dead in a windmill near Rooks Hill on the Sussex Downs, and on Hindhead one of the bodies on the gibbet was beaten down to the ground.

Moles work, and heave up their hillocks.

December 24

My great parlour turns out a fine warm winter-room, and affords a pleasant equal warmth. In blustering weather the chimney smokes a little till the shaft becomes hot. The chief fault that I find is the strong echo, which, when many people are talking, makes confusion to my poor dull ears.

December 25

Dark and mild . . . . The boys at Farringdon play in the churchyard in their shirts.

December 26

A fox ran up the street at noonday.

December 27

While many other insects must be sought after in fields and woods, and waters, the *gryllus domesticus*, or house-cricket, resides altogether within our dwellings, intruding itself upon our notice whether we will or not. This species delights in new-built houses, being, like the spider, pleased with the moisture of the walls; and besides, the softness of the mortar enables them to burrow and mine between the joints of the bricks and stones, and to open communications from one room to another. They are particularly fond of kitchens and bakers' ovens, on account of their perpetual warmth. Tender insects that live abroad either enjoy only the short period of one summer, or else doze away the cold uncomfortable months in profound slumbers; but these, residing as it were in a torrid zone, are always alert and merry: a good Christmas fire is to them like the heats of the dog-days. Though they are frequently heard by day, yet is their natural time of motion only in the night. As soon as it grows dusk, the chirping increases, and they come running forth, and are from the size of a flea to that of their full stature. As one should suppose from the burning atmosphere which they inhabit, they are a thirsty race, and show great propensity for liquids, being found frequently drowned in pans of water, milk, broth, or the like. Whatever is moist they affect; and therefore often gnaw holes in wet woollen stockings and aprons that are hung to the fire: they are the housewife's barometer, foretelling her when it will rain; and are prognostic sometimes, she thinks, of ill or good luck; of the death of a near relation, or the approach of an absent lover. By being the constant companion of her solitary hours they naturally become the objects of her superstition.

December 28

A *musca domestica*, by the warmth of my parlour, has lengthened his life and existence to this time. He usually basks on the jambs of the chimney within the influence of the fire after dinner, and settles on the table, where he sips the wine and tastes the sugar and baked apples. If there comes a very severe day he withdraws and is not seen.

December 29

Some snow in the night. Carried some savoy head, endive and celery into the cellar. The potatoes have been there some days.

December 30

Papilio Io [peacock butterfly] appears within doors, and is very brisk.

December 31

It froze under people's beds. Great rimes, and beautiful sunny days.

GILBERT WHITE'S WRITINGS

GILBERT WHITE'S *Natural History and Antiquities of Selborne [NHS]*, which consists in the main of a series of letters addressed to Thomas Pennant and the Honourable Daines Barrington, first appeared in 1788 (title-page post-dated 1789). Many subsequent editions have been published, among them a facsimile edition issued in 1970. The chapters on Antiquities are generally omitted from modern editions of the book.

White's other literary remains were all published posthumously. *The Garden Kalendar [GK]*, written between the years 1751 and 1767, was first published in full in Volume I of R. Bowdler Sharpe's edition of the *Natural History and Antiquities of Selborne*, 1900. (The second volume of Thomas Bell's edition of the *Natural History and Antiquities of Selborne*, 1877, prints only extracts from the *Kalendar*.) A facsimile edition of the *Garden Kalendar* appeared in 1975. The *Flora Selborniensis [FS]*, compiled during the year 1766, was published in 1911 as *A Nature Calendar by Gilbert White* (edited by Wilfred M. Webb). Extensive extracts from the *Naturalist's Journal [NJ]* that White kept between 1768 and 1793 were edited by Walter Johnson in a volume entitled *The Journals of Gilbert White* (1931; reprinted 1970 and 1982). Francesca Greenoak's edition of *The Journals of Gilbert White* (three volumes, 1986–9) reprints the *Garden Kalendar* and *Flora Selborniensis*, and provides the full text of the *Naturalist's Journal*. White's letters to correspondents other than Pennant and Barrington can be found in R. Holt-White's *Life and Letters of Gilbert White of Selborne* (two volumes, 1901).

The dates and (in abbreviated form) sources of the passages quoted in the present volume are as follows:

JANUARY 1: NJ 1784; **2**: NJ 1786, 1775, NHS (TP XLI); **3**: NJ 1789, 1786; **4**: NJ 1768, NHS (DB LXIII); **5**: NJ 1786; **6**: NJ 1786; **7**: letter to Molly White 1784; **8**: NJ 1785; **9**: NJ 1768, NHS (TP XLI); **10**: NJ 1789; **11**: NJ 1789, GK 1763; **12**: NJ 1768; **13**: NJ 1792, 1776; **14**: NJ 1776; **15**: 1789; **16**: NHS (TP XLI); **17**: NJ 1770, NHS (DB XLIII); **18**: NHS (DB LXII); **19**: NJ 1788; **20**: NJ 1776, 1775; **21**: NJ 1776; **22**: GK 1765, letter to Mary Barker 1783; **23**: NJ 1785, GK 1756; **24**: GK 1761; **25**: NJ 1771; **26**: NJ 1777, NHS (DB XVII); **27**: NJ 1782, NHS (TP V); **28**: NJ 1788; **29**: NJ 1784; **30**: GK 1758; **31**: NJ 1773.

FEBRUARY 1: NJ 1785; **2**: NJ 1787; **3**: NJ 1772; **4**: NHS (TP XLI & DB V); **5**: NJ 1790; **6**: NJ 1781; **7**: GK 1764; **8**: NJ 1782; **9**: NJ 1783, 1792; **10**: NJ 1783, 1770; **11**: NJ 1780; **12**: NHS (DB IX); **13**: NJ 1778; **14**: NJ 1783; **15**: GK 1763; **16**: NJ 1774, 1793; **17**: NJ 1779; **18**: NJ 1786; **19**: NJ 1793; **20**: letter to Molly White 1783; **21**: NJ 1789, NHS (DB LVI); **22**: FS 1766; **23**: NJ 1793; **24**: GK 1758; **25**: NJ 1775, letter to Thomas Barker 1776; **26**: NJ 1789; **27**: NJ 1781; **28**: NJ 1775, 1779; **29**: NJ 1780.

MARCH 1: GK 1766; **2**: NJ 1771; **3**: NHS (DB XLI); **4**: NJ 1771; **5**: NJ 1791, GK 1763; **6**: NJ 1768, NHS (DB XLIII); **7**: NJ 1785; **8**: NHS (DB XLV); **9**: letter to Molly White 1785, NJ 1769; **10**: GK 1759, 1752; **11**: NJ 1783; **12**: NJ 1775, *ibid.*; **13**: GK 1755; **14**: NJ 1775, NHS (TP XI); **15**: GK 1755; **16**: NJ 1780; **17**: NJ 1791, 1786; **18**: NJ 1775; **19**: NJ 1791; **20**: letter to Robert Marsham 1792; **21**: NJ 1769; **22**: GK 1756; **23**: NJ 1775, NHS (DB XXXV); **24**: NJ 1791; **25**: letter to Molly White 1786, GK 1758; **26**: NJ 1790; **27**: NJ 1774; **28**: NJ 1768; **29**: FS 1766, GK 1765; **30**: NJ 1785, 1770; **31**: GK 1756, NJ 1783.

APRIL 1: NJ 1776; **2**: NJ 1775; **3**: NJ 1787; **4**: NHS (TP VII); **5**: NJ 1793, 1784; **6**: NJ 1793, 1790; **7**: NJ 1775; **8**: NJ 1782; **9**: GK 1766; **10**: NJ 1773; **11**: NJ 1774, 1779; **12**: letter to Molly White 1779; **13**: NHS (TP XXIV); **14**: FS 1766, NJ 1788; **15**: NJ 1785; **16**: NJ 1770; **17**: letter to Samuel Barker 1786; **18**: NHS (TP XVI); **19**: NJ 1783, 1776; **20**: NJ 1789, 1790; **21**: NJ 1788, NHS (DB XIII); **22**: Antiquities of Selborne (letter V); **23**: NJ 1787, 1790; **24**: GK 1762; **25**: FS 1766, NJ 1779; **26**: NJ 1781; **27**: NJ 1774; **28**: GK 1766, FS 1766; **29**: NJ 1781, 1780; **30**: letter to Molly White 1783, GK 1763.

MAY 1: NJ 1779; **2**: GK 1759, letter to Rev. John White 1777; **3**: NJ 1793; **4**: NJ 1778, 1776, 1784; **5**: GK 1759; **6**: NJ 1791; **7**: NJ 1791; **8**: GK 1766; **9**: NJ 1790,1793; **10**: NJ 1790; **11**: NJ 1791, GK 1763; **12**: NJ 1776; **13**: NJ 1781, 1789; **14**: NJ 1784, NHS (DB XVIII); **15**: NJ 1789, 1788; **16**: NJ 1774, NHS (DB XVI); **17**: NJ 1786; **18**: NJ 1786; **19**: NJ 1786, NHS (TP XXI); **20**: NJ 1792; **21**: NJ 1784; **22**:

NJ 1784, letter to Molly White 1784; **23**: NJ 1785, NHS (DB XIV); **24**: FS 1766; **25**: NJ 1791; **26**: NJ 1777, NHS (TP XVI); **27**: FS 1766, NJ 1774; **28**: NJ 1784, letter to Molly White 1784; **29**: NJ 1793; **30**: NJ 1778, NHS (TP XI); **31**: NJ 1792.

JUNE 1: NJ 1791, 1790; **2**: NJ 1770, 1784; **3**: NJ 1790, 1791; **4**: NJ 1769, NHS (DB XXVII); **5**: NJ 1777; **6**: NJ 1775, NHS (DB XXI), NJ 1774; **7**: NJ 1772, NHS (DB XLVI); **8**: NJ 1772, 1759; **9**: NJ 1782, 1775; **10**: NJ 1778, 1771; **11**: NJ 1773, 1789; **12**: NJ 1780; **13**: NJ 1788; **14**: NJ 1778; **15**: NJ 1782, NHS (DB VII); **16**: NJ 1784, 1781; **17**: NJ 1788, 1792; **18**: NJ 1788, GK 1766; **19**: GK 1765, NJ 1788; **20**: NJ 1782, 1778; **21**: GK 1765, 1761; **22**: NJ 1788, 1792, 1777, NHS (DB XVIII); **23**: NJ 1788; **24**: NHS (TB XXVII); **25**: NJ 1785, 1786, 1792; **26**: letter to Rev. John White 1776; **27**: NJ 1788, 1792; **28**: NJ 1782; **29**: NJ 1774, NHS (DB XVIII); **30**: GK 1759.

JULY 1: letter to Samuel Barker 1776; **2**: NJ 1780; **3**: NJ 1778; **4**: NJ 1773, 1784; **5**: NHS (DB XXI); **6**: NJ 1792, NHS (TP XXII), GK 1765; **7**: NJ 1781, NHS (DB XVIII); **8**: NJ 1782, NHS (DB XIV); **9**: NJ 1788, *ibid.*; **10**: NJ 1784; **11**: NJ 1783, 1772; **12**: NJ 1778; **13**: GK 1765, NJ 1786, 1778; **14**: NHS (TP VIII); **15**: NJ 1786; **16**: NJ 1785; **17**: NJ 1783; **18**: NJ 1777, 1781; **19**: NJ 1769, 1786; **20**: NJ 1768, NHS (DB XV); **21**: NJ 1783, 1776; **22**: NJ 1785; **23**: NJ 1770; **24**: NJ 1779; **25**: NJ 1790; **26**: NJ 1782; **27**: NHS (TP XVIII); **28**: NJ 1790, 1789; **29**: NJ 1788, GK 1765; **30**: NJ 1776, NHS (TP XXXV); **31**: NJ 1772, 1775.

AUGUST 1: NJ 1772, 1785; **2**: NJ 1782; **3**: NJ 1786; **4**: GK 1766, NHS (DB XXXI); **5**: NJ 1780; **6**: NJ 1771, NHS (TP XXXVI); **7**: NHS (DB XLII), *ibid.*; **8**: NJ 1781, *ibid.*; **9**: FS 1766, NJ 1774; **10**: NJ 1790; **11**: GK 1760; **12**: NJ 1791; **13**: NJ 1774, 1781; **14**: NJ 1790, 1791; **15**: NJ 1772; **16**: NJ 1779, 1787; **17**: GK 1765, NHS (TP XXXIV); **18**: NJ 1789, 1771; **19**: NJ 1790; **20**: NJ 1790, 1791; **21**: NJ 1784; **22**: NJ 1783, GK 1765; **23**: NJ 1781; **24**: GK 1764, 1765; **25**: NJ 1784; **26**: NJ 1787; **27**: GK 1765, NJ 1792; **28**: NJ 1786; **29**: NJ 1774, 1781; **30**: NJ 1786; **31**: NJ 1790, letter to Molly White 1784.

SEPTEMBER 1: NJ 1778; **2**: NJ 1789; **3**: NJ 1791; **4**: letter to Molly White 1781, NJ 1778; **5**: NJ 1784; **6**: NJ 1777, NHS (DB XVII), **7**: NJ 1777, NHS (DB XVIII); **8**: GK 1762; **9**: GK 1765, NHS (DB XL); **10**: GK 1768, NJ 1781; **11**: GK 1760, NJ 1783; **12**: NJ 1791; **13**: GK 1754; **14**: NJ 1790; **15**: NJ 1768, 1788; **16**: NJ 1780; **17**: NJ 1777; **18**: GK 1762; **19**: NJ 1786, NHS (DB XXIII); **20**: letter to Molly White 1785; **21**: NJ 1791, FS 1766; **22**: NJ 1771; **23**: NJ 1783, 1792; **24**: NJ 1788; **25**: NJ 1774, 1775; **26**: NJ 1785; **27**: NJ 1770, GK 1757; **28**: GK 1761; **29**: NJ 1778, NHS (TP XXVIII); **30**: GK 1765.

OCTOBER 1: NJ 1781, 1792; **2**: NJ 1787; **3**: NJ 1783, 1776; **4**: NJ 1783; **5**: NJ 1770; **6**: NJ 1784, 1775; **7**: NJ 1782, 1781; **8**: NJ 1788; **9**: NJ 1776; **10**: NJ 1783, 1777; **11**: NJ 1777; **12**: NJ 1776; **13**: NJ 1771; **14**: NJ 1786, 1789; **15**: GK 1760, NJ

1780; **16**: NJ 1 776; **17**: NJ 1778; **18**: NJ 1790; **19**: letter to Mrs Barker 1784; **20**: NJ 1775; **21**: NJ 1790; **22**: NJ 1775; **23**: NJ 1784, 1788; **24**: GK 1761; **25**: GK 1759; **26**: NJ 1782, NHS (DB LIV); **27**: NJ 1776; **28**: NJ 1774; **29**: NJ 1781; **30**: NJ 1789; **31**: NJ 1784.

NOVEMBER 1: NJ 1776; **2**: NJ 1780; **3**: NJ 1777; **4**: NJ 1790, 1774; **5**: NJ 1773, 1786; **6**: letter to Molly White 1783, GK 1765; **7**: NJ 1783, NHS (TP IX); **8**: NJ 1776; **9**: NJ 1776; **10**: NJ 1781; **11**: NJ 1774, 1787; **12**: GK 1760; **13**: NJ 1769; **14**: NJ 1777, 1782; **15**: NJ 1790; **16**: NJ 1787; **17**: NJ 1777; **18**: NJ 1786, 1782; **19**: NJ 1792; **20**: NJ 1770; **21**: GK 1754; **22**: NJ 1786; **23**: NJ 1788, letter to Samuel Barker 1780; **24**: NJ 1776, 1775; **25**: NJ 1789; **26**: NJ 1776; **27**: NJ 1782, NHS (DB L); **28**: NJ 1787; **29**: NJ 1785; **30**: NJ 1788.

DECEMBER 1: NJ 1775; **2**: NJ 1779; **3**: NJ 1789, 1788; **4**: GK 1767, NHS (TP XII & XIII); **5**: NJ 1791, 1783; **6**: NJ 1780; **7**: NJ 1788; **8**: NJ 1789; **9**: NJ 1778, NHS (DB XXIX); **10**: NJ 1792; **11**: NJ 1777; **12**: NJ 1789; **13**: NJ 1772, NHS (TP XIII); **14**: NJ 1776; **15**: NJ 1781; **16**: NJ 1788; **17**: letter to Anne Barker (undated); **18**: GK 1762; **19**: letter to Molly White 1781; **20**: NJ 1777; **21**: NJ 1776, 1775; **22**: NJ 1784; **23**: NJ 1790, 1788; **24**: letter to Mrs Barker 1778; **25**: NJ 1782; **26**: NJ 1777; **27**: NHS (DB XLVII); **28**: NJ 1787; **29**: NJ 1783; **30**: NJ 1769; **31**: GK 1767.

The wood-engravings by Bewick in this volume are taken from the *History of Quadrupeds* (first published in 1790), *British Birds* (1797–1804), *Fables of Aesop* (1818) and *Memoir of Thomas Bewick* (1862). The editor is indebted to Margaret Norwell, Librarian at the Literary and Philosophical Society of Newcastle upon Tyne, for assistance with these illustrations.